Historical American Biographies

# WILLIAM TECUMSEH SHERMAN

## Union General

Zachary Kent

**Enslow Publishers, Inc.**

| | |
|---|---|
| 40 Industrial Road | PO Box 38 |
| Box 398 | Aldershot |
| Berkeley Heights, NJ 07922 | Hants GU12 6BP |
| USA | UK |

http://www.enslow.com

**Library of Congress Cataloging-in-Publication Data**

Kent, Zachary.
  William Tecumseh Sherman: Union General /Zachary Kent.
    p. cm. — (Historical American biographies)
  Includes bibliographical references and index.
  Summary: Examines the life and career of the Union Civil War General,
most remembered for his march through Atlanta that helped the North
achieve victory.
  ISBN 0-7660-1621-8
  1. Sherman, William T. (William Tecumseh), 1820–1891—Juvenile
literature 2. Generals—United States—Biography—Juvenile literature.
3. United States. Army—Biography—Juvenile literature. 4. United
States—History—Civil War, 1861–1865—Campaigns—Juvenile literature.
[1. Sherman, William T. (William Tecumseh), 1820–1891. 2. Generals. 3.
United States—History—Civil War, 1861–1865. 4. Sherman's March to the
Sea.]  I. Title. II. Series.
  E467.1.S55 .K365 2002
  355'.0092—dc21

                                                                    2001006699

Printed in the United States of America

10 9 8 7 6 5 4 3 2 1

**To Our Readers:**
We have done our best to make sure all Internet addresses in this book were
active and appropriate when we went to press. However, the author and the pub-
lisher have no control over and assume no liability for the material available on
those Internet sites or on other Web sites they may link to. Any comments or sug-
gestions can be sent by e-mail to comments@enslow.com or to the address on the
back cover.

**Illustration Credits:** Enslow Publishers, Inc., pp. 60, 84; Reproduced
from the Collections of the Library of Congress, pp. 6, 13, 15, 50, 68,
87, 95, 103, 109; National Archives and Records Administration, pp. 4,
8, 20, 35, 42, 52, 58, 72, 76, 79, 82, 99; Reproduced from the
*Dictionary of American Portraits*, published by Dover Publications, Inc.,
in 1967, p. 64.

**Cover Illustration:** Reproduced from the Collections of the Library of
Congress (Background); National Archives and Records Administration
(Sherman Portrait).

# CONTENTS

*William Tecumseh Sherman*

# 1

# THE BURNING
# OF ATLANTA

G reat roaring sheets of flame licked the sky. Huge billowing clouds of smoke choked the air. The city of Atlanta, Georgia, was on fire on the night of November 15, 1864. Machinery crashed through charred factory floors into heaps of twisted wreckage. Brick walls sagged and tumbled down. Burning timbers cracked and popped, sending sparks spraying in all directions. Through the streets horses galloped in wild panic. The shouts of excited men only added to the frightening scene.

During the Civil War, Northern troops captured Atlanta and occupied the city for six weeks. Then the blue-clad Union men received orders to destroy everything of value to the Confederate enemy.

*After burning Atlanta, General Sherman sent his army on a march of destruction across the state of Georgia.*

Soldiers first knocked down the stone railroad roundhouse. Soon a foundry and a freight warehouse went up in flames. Through the night, the soldiers eagerly torched the city's machine shops and mills. Fires sprang up in the hotels, theaters, and dry-goods stores. Flames also quickly engulfed the Atlanta jail and slave market buildings. Union Major George Nichols exclaimed, "The air is filled with flying, burning cinders; buildings covering two hundred acres are in ruins or in flames; every instant there is the sharp . . . sound of exploding shells and powder."[1] Along the streets, gleeful soldiers broke windows.

They looted stores and private homes and then set them on fire. Before long the night glowed so brightly that in an army camp a mile and a half away a Union soldier from Minnesota claimed he could see well enough to read a newspaper at midnight.

One lean, grim Union officer, with red hair and a short, rough beard, stalked the Atlanta streets. He stared at the damage around him with special interest. Major General William Tecumseh Sherman understood the terrors of war perhaps better than any soldier in the North or South. Now, in a bold sweeping move, he intended to show the Southern people those terrors. Already, sixty-two thousand of Sherman's toughest troops waited on the Georgia roads stretching to the southeast. "All the sick and wounded men had been sent back by rail to Chattanooga [Tennessee]," Sherman later explained,

**Hollywood Burns Atlanta**

Margaret Mitchell's 1936 novel *Gone With the Wind* was a huge success. It told the Civil War story of Scarlett O'Hara and her Georgia plantation named Tara. Hollywood producer David O. Selznick bought the motion picture rights to the book. In December 1938, Selznick reproduced the burning of Atlanta on a Hollywood backlot during the filming of the movie.

*Major General William Tecumseh Sherman is pictured here seated on horseback in the outskirts of Atlanta, Georgia. On November 15, 1864, Sherman ordered the city burned.*

"all our wagon-trains had been carefully over-hauled and loaded, so as to be ready to start on an hour's notice."[2] Sherman planned to cripple the state's military resources, its farms, railroads, factories, and mills. By leading his columns on a 300-mile march of destruction all the way to Savannah and the sea, Sherman promised, "I can . . . make Georgia howl!"[3]

After the Civil War, many Southerners would curse his name and call him heartless. But William Tecumseh Sherman realized that the fastest way to end a war was to fight total war.

# THE FOSTER SON

In the early 1800s, American settlers pressed westward over the Appalachian Mountains onto traditional American-Indian lands. One American Indian, the Shawnee chief Tecumseh, rose up to lead the fight against these invaders. Many Americans grew to respect Tecumseh as a great warrior. After uniting his people, Tecumseh fought bravely, until his death at the Battle of the Thames in Canada in 1813. Charles Sherman, an Ohio settler, decided he would like to honor Tecumseh by naming a son after him.

## A Birth and a Death

Charles Sherman and his wife, Mary Hoyt Sherman, had settled in Lancaster, Ohio, in 1811. The couple already had five children, two boys and three girls, by 1820. On February 8, 1820, in the Shermans' two-story wooden house on Main Street, Mary Sherman gave birth to her sixth child. Fulfilling his wish, Charles Sherman named the red-haired baby Tecumseh Sherman. The boy was nicknamed Cump. During the years that followed, the Shermans had five more children, making a huge family of eleven children altogether.

Charles Sherman was an educated man. In Ohio, he worked as a tax collector and a lawyer. In 1823, the Ohio state legislature elected him a judge on the Ohio Supreme Court. This respected job required that he travel to courthouses in all parts of the state. One hot spring day in 1829, Judge Sherman was riding to Lebanon, Ohio, when he fell ill with a fever. For six days he lay sick in a Lebanon hotel. Doctors thought perhaps he had cholera or typhoid fever. On June 24, Judge Charles Sherman died far from his family. Maria Sherman suddenly found herself a widow with very little money to provide for her children.

## The Ewing Home

Thomas Ewing and his wife, Maria, lived in a handsome brick house at the corner of High and Main streets in Lancaster. They took an interest in the Sherman family, who lived just two blocks away.

Thomas Ewing was a successful lawyer and an old friend of Charles Sherman. He realized how difficult Mary Sherman's life was going to be. Ewing decided to take on the responsibility of raising one of the Sherman children. In the 1800s, kindhearted people sometimes helped needy friends and relatives in this way.

"I want one of them," Ewing told Mary Sherman. "You must give me the brightest of the lot, and I will make a man of him."

The child she decided to let him have was nine-year-old Tecumseh.

"I took him home," said Ewing later, "and he was, thereafter, my boy."[1]

Mary Sherman sent several of her children to live with other friends and relatives. It was the only solution the poor widow could find for taking care of them. In the Ewing house, Cump Sherman joined four Ewing children. He was already a close friend of Phil Ewing. Five-year-old Ellen Ewing long remembered the first day Sherman entered their home in June 1829: "I peeped at him with great interest."[2] In the years that followed, two more children would be born into the Ewing family, making it a lively household.

## A New Name

While the Sherman family was Protestant, the Ewing family practiced the Roman Catholic religion. Not long after young Cump's arrival in their home, the Ewings decided that the boy should be baptized. Widow Sherman did not object, and in the Ewings' front parlor a priest arrived to perform the ceremony.

The priest quickly rejected the American-Indian name Tecumseh as a proper Christian name for the boy. "He must be named for a saint," he declared. He examined a book that listed the Roman Catholic saints and soon announced, "Today is the feast of St. William, June 25. I'll name him William."[3] During his life, Sherman would resist becoming a Catholic. But as a result of this youthful baptism, his name officially became William Tecumseh Sherman.

## Ohio Boyhood

Cump felt a great love and respect for his foster father. "A better . . . man never lived," he later insisted.[4] Ohioans thought highly of Ewing, too. In 1831, the Ohio legislature elected Thomas Ewing to serve in the U.S. Senate.

When the Senate was in session, Ewing lived in the national capital, Washington, D.C. Even then he thought about his foster son. On December 9, 1831, he sent a letter home to his wife: ". . . And there is Cumpy too—he is disposed to be bashful, not quite at home. . . . Inspire him with confidence and make him feel one of the family."[5]

Whenever Ewing was in Lancaster, he often worked late in his backyard law office. Cump and his foster brother Phil often stayed up to tend the fire for him. In addition, Cump performed many other household chores. He chopped firewood, milked the cow, and walked to the post office for the mail. Thomas Ewing recalled, "I never knew so young a boy who would do an errand so correctly and promptly as he did. He was . . . honest, faithful and reliable."[6]

Around 1832, two brothers, Sam and John Howe, took over the local school, Lancaster Academy. Seated at his wooden desk, Cump studied hard. He eagerly read every book he could get his hands on, including the plays of William Shakespeare and the novels of Sir Walter Scott. He also loved to write, and one friend remembered seeing him only "rarely . . . without

*William Tecumseh Sherman's foster father Thomas Ewing (pictured) served many years as a U.S. senator from Ohio. In 1849, President Zachary Taylor would name Ewing as the nation's first secretary of the interior.*

a pen in his hand."[7] Cump's friends often teased him about his red hair, calling him "Red-headed Woodpecker."[8]

Cump took his first paying job in 1834. That autumn and the next spring, he worked with a surveying party. The surveyors carefully measured the land and prepared the route of the Great Ohio Canal south through Lancaster to the Ohio River. Young Cump earned a silver half-dollar for each day's work.

## A Military Education

As a U.S. senator, Thomas Ewing had the power to appoint two cadets to the United States Military Academy at West Point, New York, each year. Ewing decided his growing foster son should get an education there. On August 1, 1835, Ewing wrote to Secretary of War Lewis Cass praising Cump Sherman as "a stout athlete . . . a good Latin, Greek & French scholar & very good . . . in the Mathematics."[9] In the spring of 1836, sixteen-year-old Cump received his appointment to West Point.

Twelve-year-old Ellen Ewing watched her foster brother climb into a stagecoach that May. She remembered him as "a tall, slim, loosely jointed boy with red hair, fair burned skin and piercing black eyes."[10] The stagecoach bounced along rutted roads until it reached a railroad station at Frederick,

Maryland. Finally, on June 1, 1836, Cump arrived at the boardinghouse where Senator Ewing lived when in Washington. He briefly visited with Ewing, and the senator soon wrote to his wife, "I have great confidence that Cumpy will make a man that we shall be proud of. . . . He is a fine boy."[11]

## West Point Cadet

Cump Sherman continued his journey northward and finally arrived at West Point on the Hudson River in June 1836. He passed his entrance examinations easily and soon joined 115 other boys as a new military cadet.

*United States Military Academy cadets march on the parade ground at West Point, New York. While an excellent classroom student, Cadet Sherman often disobeyed military rules.*

Cadet Cump Sherman quickly learned military academy routine. The blare of a bugle awakened him at dawn each morning. Through the day he studied in class and drilled on the field. Cump was a good student, but even he admitted, "I was not considered a good soldier."[12] Cadets received points called demerits for every mistake they made. Cump got demerits for such things as speaking in ranks, visiting another cadet's room after hours, tardiness, and poorly shined shoes. He received an average of one hundred fifty demerits each year he was at West Point. Students with more than two hundred demerits in a year were asked to leave the academy.

### Future Generals

Cump Sherman made many friends at West Point who later played important roles in the Civil War. One of his best friends, classmate George H. Thomas, rose to the command of the Union Army of the Cumberland. Friends P.G.T. Beauregard and Irvin McDowell were in the class two years ahead of Cump. As commanding generals, Beauregard and McDowell would fight one another at the Battle of Bull Run in 1861. Perhaps the most important of Cump's fellow cadets was another Ohio boy, Ulysses S. Grant. Grant arrived at West Point as a freshman when Cump was a senior. The bashful Grant grew to become General in Chief of all the Union armies.

Cadet William S. Rosecrans recalled, "Sherman . . . was one of the most popular and brightest fellows in the academy. . . . He was considered the best hash-maker at West Point."[13] Cadets gathered for secret late-night parties in Cump Sherman's room. He expertly mashed potatoes and mixed in pepper, salt, and butter to make a tasty dish for frying over the open fireplace. As they ate, the cadets joked, told stories, and bragged of glorious futures as army officers.

After four years at West Point, twenty-year-old William Tecumseh Sherman ranked sixth among the forty-three cadets in his graduating class. On July 1, 1840, he proudly received his commission as a second lieutenant in the U.S. Army.

# SOLDIER AND CIVILIAN

"I have a natural curiosity to see strange places and people, both of which exist in Florida," William Tecumseh Sherman wrote to his foster mother.[1] In October 1840, Lieutenant Sherman joined Company A of the Third Artillery Regiment. The regiment was stationed at Fort Pierce on the east coast of Florida along the Indian River.

## The Seminole War

Since 1836 the U.S. Army had been at war against Florida's Seminole Indians, in order to gain complete control of the territory. Although there were few remaining Seminole warriors, they stubbornly escaped capture by hiding in the Florida swamps.

Lieutenant Sherman assisted in rounding up some of the Seminole. In May 1841, he received orders to capture the Seminole chief Coacoochee, nicknamed Wild Cat. Sherman boldly trotted alone on horseback into the Seminole camp. His squad of soldiers followed at a distance. He called upon Coacoochee to surrender with his few warriors. While talking, Sherman secretly signaled to his soldiers to seize the Seminole rifles that were leaning against a tree. Suddenly defenseless, the warriors surrendered, and Sherman successfully returned to Fort Pierce with his prisoners. In March 1842, military officials declared the costly Seminole War over because it was not worth battling the few remaining Seminoles. No treaty was ever signed, and several hundred Seminole remained hiding in the swamps.

## New Assignments

On November 30, 1841, Sherman received a promotion to first lieutenant. During the next six months, Sherman's Company A served near St. Augustine, Florida, as well as at Fort Morgan, Alabama. Then, in June 1842, he was ordered to Fort Moultrie on Sullivan's Island in the harbor of Charleston, South Carolina. Sherman enjoyed Charleston's high society. He galloped horseback on fox hunts and danced in his dress uniform at grand parties. In Charleston Harbor he watched laborers at work constructing the new Fort Sumter.

In the autumn of 1843, he traveled home to Lancaster on three months' leave, his first vacation in three years. Since leaving home for West Point, Sherman had often exchanged letters with his foster sister Ellen Ewing. Their close friendship gradually blossomed into romance. Now, sitting hand in hand, they agreed to become engaged. Ellen's parents approved. Ellen urged him to become a Catholic, quit the army, and go to work for her father. Senator

*A view of Fort Moultrie, South Carolina, where Lieutenant Sherman was stationed from 1842 to 1846. Sherman grew very fond of the region and made many close friends while living in the South.*

Ewing owned an Ohio saltworks where salty marsh water was boiled into salt. He wanted Sherman to become the manager. But Sherman resisted all of these ideas. "I would rather earn my living by the labor of my own hands," he told her.[2]

Sherman returned to duty after his leave ended. In February 1844, he journeyed to Marietta, Georgia, to investigate claims for back pay by some Seminole War veterans. While in northern Georgia, Sherman took time to explore the area. On long horseback rides he studied the geography until he knew it by heart. He returned to Fort Moultrie in the spring of 1844.

## War With Mexico

American settlers in the Mexican region called Texas had declared their independence from Mexico in 1836. The Texans won their fight for freedom, and in 1845, Texas joined the United States as the twenty-eighth state. But since 1836, Texans and Mexicans had continued to argue about their border. Many Americans believed it was the obvious fate of the United States to continue expanding westward until the country reached from the Atlantic to the Pacific oceans. They called this national policy Manifest Destiny, and would let nothing stand in their way. In April 1846, cannons roared along the Rio Grande as the Mexican War erupted. In May, Sherman reported for duty at Pittsburgh, Pennsylvania. It was his job to organize volunteers who were rushing south to join the fight.

At the battles of Palo Alto and Resaca de la Palma in May 1846, U.S. General Zachary Taylor won stunning victories. Sherman yearned to get into the fighting like so many of his West Point classmates. Finally, in June, he excitedly learned he was to report for duty in the Mexican territory of California.

## To California by Sea

On July 13, 1846, Sherman sailed from New York City aboard the USS *Lexington*. West Point friend Captain Henry W. Halleck was aboard the ship, too. "We soon settled down to the humdrum of a long voyage," Sherman explained, "reading some . . . playing games . . . and . . . eating our meals regularly."[3]

The *Lexington* stopped at Rio de Janeiro, Brazil, in September. Then it sailed around Cape Horn at the southern tip of South America through windy ice storms. At last the ship sailed into Monterey Bay, California, on January 26, 1847. After a voyage of 198 days, Sherman recalled, "Every thing [sic] on the shore looked bright and beautiful, the hills covered with grass and flowers."[4]

All the fighting in California had ended by the time Sherman arrived. General Stephen W. Kearny commanded the conquered territory as military governor. Taking up his duties as a quartermaster at Monterey, Sherman supervised the building of sawmills and gristmills. It was his job to make the army post self-supporting. While war still raged in Mexico, Sherman found the calm of California frustrating. He wrote to Ellen: "There is nothing new here. No strange events . . . no battles . . . no nothing and this war will pass and I will have to blush and say I have not heard a hostile shot."[5]

## A Discovery at Sutter's Mill

Colonel Richard B. Mason eventually replaced Kearny as military governor of California. Mason made Sherman an aide on his staff. One day in the late spring of 1848, the colonel called Sherman into his Monterey office. Two American settlers had brought him some yellow rocks from the American Fork River where landowner John Sutter was building a sawmill.

"What is that?" Mason asked Sherman.

Sherman examined the rocks and responded with a surprised question, "Is it gold?"[6]

Gold had been discovered at Sutter's Mill, and the news quickly spread throughout the region. Sherman excitedly persuaded Colonel Mason to let him journey up to Sutter's Mill and investigate the situation. Along the American Fork River, Sherman saw some four thousand men eagerly digging with picks and shovels. They were finding as much as fifty thousand dollars' worth of gold a day. When he returned to Monterey, Sherman wrote a report, which Colonel Mason sent east to Washington. It was the first official news of the California gold strike.

## Special Messenger

In March 1848, the Mexican War ended with the signing of the Treaty of Guadalupe Hidalgo. In exchange for $15 million, the defeated Mexicans gave the United States all of the land north of the Rio Grande. This included the California and New Mexico territories (the present-day states of California, Nevada, Utah, Arizona, New Mexico, and parts of Wyoming, Colorado, Kansas, Oklahoma, and Texas).

In California, Major General Persifor F. Smith replaced Mason in February 1849. Smith moved the army headquarters from Monterey to San Francisco. The California Gold Rush brought miners hurrying into the territory. "During the summer of 1849," Sherman recalled, "there continued to pour into California a perfect stream of people. Steamers came. . . . Wharves were built, houses were springing up as if by magic. . . ."[7]

General Smith decided to send Sherman east to deliver some military letters. Sherman departed on the steamer *Oregon* on January 2, 1850. Instead of sailing around the tip of South America, this time he crossed overland at Panama. Using this new but exhausting and dangerous jungle route, the trip took only thirty days. Sherman reached New York City at the end of January.

After reporting to General Winfield Scott in New York City, Sherman continued south to see Secretary of War George W. Crawford in Washington. The Ewing family was living at the Blair House in Washington. The mansion stood on Pennsylvania Avenue near the White House. President Zachary Taylor had named Thomas Ewing to his Cabinet as the first Secretary of the Interior. Secretary Ewing was in charge of government-owned land, the Bureau of Indian Affairs, the government pension office, and the patent office.

The Ewings warmly welcomed Sherman, and he and Ellen made their wedding plans. The marriage of thirty-year-old William Tecumseh Sherman and twenty-six-year-old Ellen Ewing took place on May 1, 1850. Three hundred guests jammed into Blair House to watch the ceremony. President Taylor, Cabinet members, and famous senators Daniel Webster and Henry Clay all stepped forward to kiss the bride.

At the end of their honeymoon to Niagara Falls, New York, the newlyweds returned to Washington in time for the Fourth of July celebrations. Sadly, President Taylor fell ill that hot summer day with cholera or typhoid fever. On July 9, Taylor died, and Vice President Millard Fillmore suddenly became president. As a courtesy to the new president, to let him select his own Cabinet members, Thomas Ewing resigned as Secretary of the Interior. The Ohio legislature promptly elected him a senator again.

## San Francisco Banker

In September 1850, Sherman was promoted to the rank of captain. He joined Company C of the Third Artillery Regiment at Jefferson Barracks, Missouri, near St. Louis. The Shermans' first child, Maria ("Minnie"), was born in January 1851. A second daughter, Mary Elizabeth ("Lizzie"), was born in November 1852.

As a commissary officer at Jefferson Barracks, Sherman bought cattle and other food supplies for the army post. He explained to Ellen, however, "I am getting tired of this dull, tame life."[8] One of Sherman's old army friends, Major Henry S. Turner, had become a banker. Turner and his partners wished to establish a bank in San Francisco and hire Sherman to be its manager. Sherman carefully considered the offer. He even took another trip out to California to study the situation. Only three thousand people had lived in San Francisco, California, when he had left in 1850. California had become a state that same year. In April 1853, he saw fifty thousand people crowding the muddy streets. "San Francisco is quite a large city now," he marveled.[9]

Sherman accepted Turner's offer. He would manage the San Francisco branch of Lucas & Turner for a salary of five thousand dollars and one eighth of all the bank's profits. On September 6, 1853, thirty-three-year-old Sherman resigned from the army. Ellen Sherman arrived with little Lizzie that summer. Minnie remained behind with her grandparents in Lancaster. In June 1854, the Shermans welcomed a new baby into the family when their first son, William, was born.

San Francisco brought Lucas & Turner success. Sherman built a new bank building on the corner of Jackson and Montgomery streets. California settlers put their money into the bank and deposits soon rose to five hundred thousand dollars. Then suddenly a financial panic struck the city on February 22, 1855. Without reason, people feared their money was unsafe in banks. Sherman recalled, "Rumors from the street came pouring in that Wright & Co. had failed; then Wells, Fargo & Co.; then Palmer, Cook & Co., and indeed all, or nearly all, the banks of the city."[10] People worried that Sherman's bank would close its doors, too. Sherman remained calm throughout the crisis. He paid out money to every nervous depositor who demanded it. Although he had to pay out $417,000, Lucas & Turner was able to survive the danger.

## Hard-Luck Banker

On October 12, 1856, Ellen Sherman gave birth to a fourth child, Thomas Ewing Sherman. That autumn, Henry Turner and his St. Louis partners decided to close the San Francisco bank. They intended to open a bank in New York City instead and asked Sherman to manage it. The Sherman family boarded the ship *Sonora* and journeyed to New York. In July 1857, Sherman established a new bank called Lucas & Symonds at 12 Wall Street. Within days, the financial Panic of 1857 struck nationwide. Political tensions in Europe made people fearful of the future world economy. Many anxious Americans decided their money was unsafe in banks. The demands of worried depositors proved too much this time. The New York bank was forced to close.

While a banker, Sherman had made some poor investments for a number of his army friends. With a sense of honor, he eventually paid these debts out of his own pocket. Sherman had experienced nothing but bad luck in the banking business. He told his wife, "I regret I ever left the Army."[11]

**Two Out-of-Luck Ex-Soldiers**

While visiting St. Louis on bank business, Sherman ran into another unlucky West Pointer, Ulysses S. Grant. Grant had fought in the Mexican War and had risen to the rank of captain. But now he could earn a living only as a farmer and woodcutter. Sherman later recalled thinking, "West Point and the regular army were not good schools for farmers [and] bankers."[12]

## On the Kansas Plains

"Mr. Ewing has set his mind on having me in Kansas, and I . . . respect his wishes," Sherman wrote to a friend.[13] Thomas Ewing wanted Sherman to manage some Kansas real estate he owned. At the same time, Sherman's foster brothers Hugh and Thomas Ewing, Jr., offered to make him a partner in their Leavenworth, Kansas, law firm. At the end of August 1858, Sherman traveled to Leavenworth. "We had an office on Main Street, between Shawnee and Delaware, on the second floor," he later recalled.[14] Sherman and Hugh Ewing sold real estate, while Tom Ewing handled the legal practice.

That spring, Sherman went to work clearing his foster father's land on Indian Creek, in Shawnee County, forty miles from Leavenworth. He chopped down trees, built log cabins, and planted orchards. "I am doomed to be a vagabond," he sadly admitted, "and shall no longer struggle against my fate."[15]

In desperation, on June 11, 1859, thirty-nine-year-old Sherman wrote to an old army friend, Major Don Carlos Buell, on duty at the War Department. He asked Buell to help him find an army position. Buell soon wrote back. He had learned that a state military college was being organized in Louisiana. He advised Sherman to apply for the job of superintendent, the overall supervisor of the school. George Mason Graham, half brother of the Colonel Mason who had been Sherman's commander in California, was on the selection committee. Sherman decided to apply for the job.

"In July, 1859, I received notice . . . that I had been elected superintendent of the proposed college," Sherman revealed.[16] The school would pay him thirty-five hundred dollars a year. In those days, a skilled laborer such as a carpenter rarely made as much as one thousand dollars a year. On September 5, Ellen gave birth to their fifth child, Eleanor ("Elly"). Sherman needed the money for his family, and he wanted the job. So late in October 1859, he set off for Louisiana.

# 4

# THE NATION
# TORN IN TWO

Located in a pine forest near Alexandria, Louisiana, the Louisiana Military Seminary first opened its doors on January 1, 1860. Sherman was not only the superintendent and treasurer of the new college. He also taught geography and American history. Superintendent Sherman gave each of his sixty students strict but kind attention. "If a cadet fell sick . . .," recalled Professor David F. Boyd, "he was at the bedside several times a day and at night."[1]

When the first school term ended, Sherman spent the summer months in the North. By the time he returned to Louisiana in October 1860, the threat of war was near.

## On the Brink of Civil War

For over forty years, the question of slavery had pushed the United States toward civil war. In the North, thousands of European immigrants gladly took jobs in busy factories. Across the Northern states, railroads carried goods from one industrial city to another. Hardy farmers tended crops on small farms. Most Northerners had no use for slavery, and many considered it to be cruel and immoral. Southerners, however, relied heavily on farm income. Cotton, tobacco, and rice were the major Southern crops. They were grown on farms and large plantations worked by African slaves. Many Southerners depended on slave labor to make their farming economy successful. As they moved westward into new U.S. territories, many Southerners wanted to bring slavery with them.

The problem reached a crisis when Abraham Lincoln was elected sixteenth president of the United States in November 1860. Angry Southerners feared that Lincoln, a Northerner from Illinois, planned to abolish slavery. They insisted that the federal government had no right to force laws on the Southern states. On December 20, 1860, South Carolina seceded from the United States (also called the Union). In the following weeks, Mississippi, Alabama, Florida, Georgia, and Texas also left the Union. Louisiana joined these rebellious states on January 26, 1861. Together they formed the Confederate States of America and chose Jefferson Davis as their president.

Sherman had spent many years living in the South. He liked the Southern people. But his first loyalty was to the nation. "I cannot bear the idea of being opposed to Uncle Sam. . . ." he insisted, "I will do no act, breathe no word, think no thought hostile to the government of the United States."[2] At the end of January, Sherman sadly wrote his resignation as superintendent of the Louisiana Military Seminary. He returned north by train to Lancaster, Ohio.

**A Visit to Washington**

Sherman's younger brother, John, was a successful Ohio politician, serving as a U.S. congressman from 1854 to 1861. In 1861, he was elected to the U.S. Senate. Sherman visited his brother in Washington in March 1861. John Sherman took him to the White House to meet President Lincoln.

"Ah," Lincoln cheerfully asked, when he learned Sherman had just come from Louisiana, "how are they getting along down there?"

"They think they are getting along [fine]," Sherman grimly told him, "They are preparing for war."[3]

## Railroad President

Sherman's old friend Henry Turner found him a new job in St Louis. For a salary of two thousand dollars a year, Sherman accepted the position of president of the Fifth Street Railroad Company. It was a city streetcar company, and horses pulled the passenger cars on rails. The Sherman family arrived in St. Louis on March 20, 1861. Sherman set to work and skillfully reduced company costs.

On April 12, 1861, Confederate cannons bombarded Fort Sumter in the Charleston, South Carolina, harbor. Two days later, the fort surrendered. Immediately, President Lincoln called for military volunteers to put down the Southern rebellion. Within days, the slave states of Virginia, Arkansas, North Carolina, and Tennessee seceded from the Union and joined the Confederacy. The Civil War had begun.

Sherman let his military friends in Washington know that he wanted to serve the North. In May, a War Department telegram informed him that he had been appointed a colonel in the U.S. Army. Sherman promptly resigned from his job and sent his family to Lancaster. Then he hurried to duty in Washington.

## Colonel Sherman

Sherman was assigned command of a newly formed brigade of thirty-four hundred volunteers. The brigade included the 13th New York, the 69th New York, the 79th New York, the 2nd Wisconsin, and the 3rd U.S. Artillery regiments. During June and July of 1861, Sherman trained his troops constantly, until his voice grew hoarse from shouting orders.

From Lancaster, word reached him that his sixth child, a daughter named Rachel, was born on July 5. He had little time to celebrate. The Confederates had made Richmond, Virginia, their capital. Northerners cried out "On to Richmond!" and demanded the capture of the city. At last, commanding Union General Irvin McDowell ordered a general advance south into Virginia. On July 15, Sherman's brigade joined the Union march.

Twenty miles to the south, General P.G.T. Beauregard commanded a Confederate army near Manassas, Virginia. It was encamped beside a stream called Bull Run. On July 18, Sherman's division commander,

*John Sherman was an Ohio congressman in the House of Representatives during the 1850s and became a U.S. senator in 1861. He kept his brother William Tecumseh informed about politics in Washington.*

Brigadier General Daniel Tyler, ordered troops across the shallow water of a ford called Blackburn's Ford on Bull Run. When Confederate soldiers fired on these men, Tyler called on Sherman's brigade for support. "For the first time in my life," Sherman declared, "I saw cannon-balls [sic] strike men and crash through the trees and saplings above and around us."[4] Having discovered the center of the Confederate defense line, Tyler pulled back.

## The Battle of Bull Run

Union General McDowell was ready to attack across Bull Run on July 21. It was the duty of Sherman's brigade, as part of Tyler's division, to hold the center of the Union line. Meanwhile, most of the Union Army circled west around the Confederate left flank several miles away. McDowell's attack from that direction caught the enemy by surprise.

Sherman and his brigade waited until noon for orders to join the raging fight. Then he led his men wading across Bull Run. The brigade rushed ahead, driving the Confederates backward up a high rise called Henry Hill. The struggle for Henry Hill soon became one of complete confusion. One by one Sherman sent his regiments attacking up the high slope. Unfortunately, the 2nd Wisconsin troops wore gray uniforms like most of the Southern soldiers.

Because of this, they were fired on by friends and enemies alike, and they fell back badly bloodied. Sherman next ordered the 79th New York Regiment into the fray. Colonel James Cameron, brother of the Secretary of War, dropped from his horse, shot dead. Sherman shouted for the 69th New York Regiment to join the charge. He spurred his horse and rode among them. "I was under heavy fire for hours," he later exclaimed, "[and] cannot imagine how I escaped."[5] One bullet grazed his knee. Another nicked his shoulder. Even after his horse was shot out from under him, he continued yelling orders.

Late in the afternoon, Confederate reinforcements arrived on the battlefield. They proved too much for the exhausted Yankees (another name for Northerners). The Northern soldiers suddenly broke and ran in wild panic. Sherman brought his brigade off the battlefield in fair order. Through the night they retreated, all the way back to Washington. "A slow, mizzling rain had set in, and probably a more gloomy day never presented itself," Sherman recalled.[6] At the bridge and ferry crossings across the Potomac River into Washington, Sherman took charge. He began to reorganize the weary, defeated troops before he allowed them into the city.

## The Stress of Command

President Lincoln recognized Sherman's skills as an army officer. On August 3, 1861, he promoted Sherman to the rank of brigadier general. Not long afterward, Major General Robert Anderson called Sherman west to join him in defending Kentucky. "I had been a lieutenant in Captain Anderson's company, at Fort Moultrie, from 1843 to 1846," Sherman recalled, "and he explained that he wanted me as his right hand."[7]

Sherman gladly agreed to serve with General Anderson. Just two months later, however, Anderson resigned because of poor health. As second in command, Sherman suddenly found himself in charge of the entire Kentucky military department. Worry over the lack of troops, equipment, and training soon wore on Sherman's nerves. Newspaper reporter Henry Villard remembered seeing Sherman at his headquarters in Louisville, Kentucky: "He lived at the Galt House [hotel] on the ground floor, and he paced the corridor outside his rooms for hours."[8]

On October 17, Secretary of War Simon Cameron visited Sherman at the Galt House. "He asked if everything was not well with us," Sherman noted, "and I told him . . . that things were . . . as bad as bad could be."[9] Sherman had eighteen thousand men under his command, but he insisted that he needed two hundred thousand. It seemed like a staggering number at that point in the war. Cameron threw up his hands and exclaimed, "Great God! where are they to come from?"[10] Sherman's nervous behavior and his demand for two hundred thousand troops caused rumors to spread that he might be crazy. In Washington, Assistant Secretary of War Thomas W. Scott remarked, "Sherman's gone in the head."[11]

## Sherman Insane?

Sherman was under such stress it seemed he was on the verge of a mental breakdown. In November, Brigadier General Don Carlos Buell arrived at Louisville and relieved Sherman of his duty. "I was transferred for duty to the Department of the Missouri," Sherman remembered, "and ordered to report in person to Major-General H.W. Halleck at St. Louis."[12]

In St. Louis, Sherman remained so clearly nervous that Ellen Sherman hurried there to nurse him. General Halleck kindly told her: "You can't work an old horse in the plough all the time. He must be turned out in the barnyard to take a rest. So take your husband home . . . for two weeks."[13]

Ellen took Sherman back to Ohio. The quiet of Lancaster helped calm him. But not long after he reached home, the *Cincinnati Commercial* newspaper printed a story with the blaring headline "GENERAL WILLIAM T. SHERMAN INSANE."[14] Other newspapers across the North reprinted the sensational article. Full of shame and fury, Sherman vowed to restore his good name.

## Organizing Troops

By Christmas 1861, Sherman had returned to duty in St. Louis. He drilled recruits at Benton Barracks, until Union General Ulysses S. Grant invaded Tennessee in February 1862. To keep Grant's army supplied, Sherman was given charge of the military supply depot at Paducah, Kentucky.

Sherman rushed men, food, and ammunition forward to Grant. On February 6, Grant captured Fort Henry and marched directly to nearby Fort Donelson. Grant was grateful for Sherman's support. "Every boat that came up with supplies or reenforcements [sic]," he explained, "brought a note of encouragement from Sherman, asking me to call upon him for any assistance he could render."[15] Fighting hard, Grant captured Fort Donelson on February 16, taking fifteen thousand Confederate prisoners. It was the first great Union victory of the war.

In March 1862, Sherman received command of a new division of volunteers he had organized at Paducah. They hurried south to join Grant's army in

Tennessee. Grant intended to concentrate his army beside the Tennessee River before marching south into Mississippi. At Pittsburg Landing, Tennessee, Sherman's troops pitched their camp in the woods near a log church called the Shiloh Meeting House. Grant's force already numbered forty thousand men, and General Buell was expected soon with another twenty-five thousand Union troops. Confederate General Albert Sidney Johnston, with an army of forty-three thousand men, was determined to make a surprise attack on Grant before Buell could arrive.

## The Battle of Shiloh

Yawning Union soldiers were just waking up on Sunday morning, April 6, 1862. At Sherman's headquarters, the colonel of the 53rd Ohio Regiment nervously reported seeing Confederate soldiers lurking in the distant woods. Sherman decided to investigate for himself. He rode to the Ohioans' campsite and peered through his binoculars into the woods. A few hundred yards away, he suddenly spied a mass of gray-clad Confederate soldiers. In an instant, the Confederates fired a rifle volley. Beside him, Sherman's orderly, Thomas D. Holliday, fell dead from his horse. "My God, we're attacked!" Sherman exclaimed.[16] The Battle of

*A view of the simple log church called the Shiloh Meeting House near Pittsburg Landing, Tennessee. A bloody battle suddenly erupted here on April 6, 1862. Ironically, Shiloh is a biblical word meaning "place of peace".*

Shiloh erupted with booming cannons and roaring musketfire.

Thousands of surprised and frightened Union troops ran away from the fight. Most of Sherman's division, however, stubbornly stood its ground, as the Confederates attacked repeatedly. Sherman galloped among his soldiers, re-forming shaken regiments and shouting commands. Cannonballs smashed into the trees around him. Bullets whistled past his ears. A piece of buckshot from a shotgun blast struck Sherman's right hand. He calmly wrapped a handkerchief around the wound. A musketball tore his shoulder strap, grazing his skin. He hardly noticed. "Tell Grant," he told a staff officer, "if he has any men to spare I can use them; if not, I will do the best I can."[17]

General Grant would never forget Sherman's brave leadership that bloody day. "During the whole of Sunday," Grant later declared, "I was continuously engaged in passing from one part of the field to another, giving directions to division commanders. In thus moving along the line, however, I never [thought] it important to stay long with Sherman."[18] In the afternoon, Confederate General Johnston bled to death when a bullet cut an artery in his leg. But by nightfall, the relentless Confederates had nearly overcome the exhausted Union Army.

## Determined Fighting

Sherman found General Grant that rainy night standing huddled under a tree. "Well, Grant," he commented, "we've had the devil's own day, haven't we?"

"Yes," Grant grimly answered, "lick 'em tomorrow, though."[19]

Grant refused to admit defeat. Through the night, General Buell's twenty-five thousand Union troops finally arrived on the battlefield. On April 7, the second day of battle, it was the Confederates' turn to be surprised. The Union Army fiercely counterattacked, and by the end of the day the Confederates retreated in confusion. In the gruesome two-day Shiloh fight, some thirteen thousand Union and eleven thousand Confederate soldiers had been killed, wounded, or captured. Sherman rode over the battlefield and never forgot the gory sight: "Wagons hauling in dead men and dumping them on the ground . . . for burial in long trenches, like sardines in a box. Wounded men with mangled legs and arms, and heads half shot off, horrible to behold."[20]

Sherman had fought heroically and proven his worth at Shiloh. On May 1, 1862, new Secretary of War Edwin Stanton, who had replaced Simon Cameron in January, announced Sherman's promotion to major general. "The battle of Shiloh," Sherman gratefully remarked, "gave me personally the chance to redeem my good name."[21]

# 5

# GENERAL OF THE XV CORPS

After the Battle of Shiloh, General Henry W. Halleck arrived to take overall command of Grant's army. General Grant, who had a reputation for drinking, was reduced to second in command. Halleck slowly advanced the army southward 24 miles to Corinth, Mississippi. On May 30, 1862, Sherman's division was among the first to march into the town, which had been abandoned by the enemy.

## Friendly Advice

Sherman found Grant one day preparing to leave camp and return home. Sherman asked him why. "Sherman," Grant replied, "you know. . . . that I am in the way here. I have stood it as long as I can, and

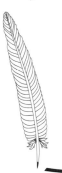

**Brother Soldiers**

Sherman and Grant developed a strong bond during the Civil War. "General Grant is a great general," Sherman insisted, "I know him well. He stood by me when I was crazy, and I stood by him when he was drunk; and now, sir, we stand by each other always."[1]

can endure it no longer."[2] Sherman urged Grant to stay. He reminded Grant that before the Battle of Shiloh, the newspapers had called him (Sherman) insane. But the battle had given Sherman a chance to prove himself. If Grant went away now, he would be forgotten. But if he stayed, some piece of good luck might restore him to favor. "He certainly appreciated my friendly advice," Sherman remembered, "and promised to wait awhile."[3]

Sure enough, on July 11, 1862, President Lincoln ordered Halleck to Washington to become General in Chief of all the Union armies. General Grant was restored to active command of the Army of the Tennessee.

## The Fight for Vicksburg

From July until December 1862, Sherman served as military governor of the western part of Tennessee with headquarters at Memphis. During that time,

Grant made plans to attack the Confederate strong-hold of Vicksburg, Mississippi. The capture of Vicksburg would give the North nearly complete control of the Mississippi River. It would cripple the South by separating Arkansas, Louisiana, and Texas from the rest of the Confederacy.

"General Sherman will command the expedition down the Mississippi," Grant explained. "He will have a force of about forty thousand men."[4] Sherman was ordered to disrupt the two railroads bringing supplies into Vicksburg. Steamboats carried Sherman's army from Memphis down the river to the mouth of the Yazoo River, eight miles above the town.

On the rainy day of December 26, Sherman's troops landed on swampy ground along the Yazoo River. Three days later, they charged the enemy positions at Chickasaw Bluffs. But the Confederate defenses proved too strong. "Dead and wounded soldiers lay . . . among the trees and bushes and others dragged themselves toward the road," Sherman gravely remembered. "The crying, groaning and sighing of the wounded was really pitiful."[5] Sherman suffered nearly two thousand men killed, wounded, or captured. "Our loss had been pretty heavy, and we had accomplished nothing," he admitted.[6]

## At Young's Point

Sherman's surviving troops reboarded the steam-
boats. On January 2, 1863, Major General John
McClernand, who outranked Sherman, arrived to
claim overall command of Sherman's troops. With
the support of navy gunboats, McClernand and
Sherman successfully attacked Confederate Fort
Hindman at Arkansas Post, Arkansas, fifty miles up
the Arkansas River. The capture of five thousand
Confederates on January 12, 1863, raised the
morale of Sherman's men. Within another week,
Sherman and McClernand joined Grant at Young's
Point, Louisiana, opposite Vicksburg.

Grant reorganized his army and gave Sherman
command of the XV Corps. The corps contained
troops from Illinois, Missouri, Iowa, and Ohio. From
January into March 1863, Grant kept Sherman's
soldiers busy digging canals. He hoped to make it
possible for river traffic to bypass Vicksburg. But
neither Grant nor Sherman expected the canals to
be successful. The flow of the Mississippi that
winter was not high enough to keep the canals filled
with water. Finally, Grant settled on a more daring
idea. A Union fleet under Admiral David D. Porter
carrying supplies and men would run directly past
the enemy cannons on the Vicksburg bluffs overlooking the river. Seven gunboats, three steamboats,
and ten barges prepared to make the attempt. "I

have no faith in the whole plan," Sherman wrote to his wife.[7] Yet he worked hard to make it succeed.

## Running Past Vicksburg

On April 16, Admiral Porter, aboard his gunboat *Benton*, led the Union fleet down the river past Vicksburg. Confederate cannonfire soon struck the steamboat *Henry Clay* and set it ablaze. "Houses on . . . shore were set on fire," recalled Sherman, "which lighted up the whole river; and the roar of cannon, the bursting of shells, and finally the burning of the *Henry Clay*, drifting with the current, made up a picture of the terrible not often seen."[8]

On April 22, six more steamers with twelve barges in tow also ran past the Vicksburg cannons. Now that he was positioned south of Vicksburg, General Grant wished to land his troops on the east bank of the Mississippi at Grand Gulf. To distract the Confederates, he sent cavalry commanded by Colonel B. H. Grierson on a raid deep into Mississippi. He also sent Sherman's XV Corps back to the Yazoo River to draw attention north of Vicksburg. On April 29, Sherman landed ten regiments of soldiers. He ordered them to tramp back and forth noisily in the woods. As a result of this trick, his force seemed much larger than it was. Confederate General John Pemberton sent

*The Union fleet runs past the fortified bluffs of Vicksburg, Mississippi, on the night of April 16, 1863. Sherman watched the exciting event from the rowboat seen at the bottom of the picture.*

reinforcements from Vicksburg rushing to the spot. By then, Sherman had retreated safely.

## Bold Maneuvers

Thanks to Sherman and Grierson, on April 30, 1863, Grant successfully landed his army at Grand Gulf 50 miles downriver from Vicksburg. Sherman's troops rejoined Grant there on May 7. Grant soon announced his intention to march his entire force of forty-three thousand men straight into enemy territory without keeping open a supply line. This was a new kind of war, and it made Sherman nervous. But he soon saw how easily the rich Mississippi countryside provided food for the army. Union soldiers raided barns, smokehouses, and cellars and carried away great quantities of meat, grain, and other food. The next time Grant visited Sherman's camp, Sherman pumped his hand. "General Grant," Sherman exclaimed, "I want to congratulate you on the success of your plan. And it's your plan, too, by heaven, nobody else's. For nobody else believed in it."[9]

Grant swiftly placed his army between Vicksburg and the Mississippi state capital of Jackson, 45 miles to the east. This movement prevented General Joseph Johnston's Confederate troops in Jackson from reinforcing General Pemberton's Vicksburg army. Sherman's XV Corps marched to Jackson and scattered Johnston's weak defensive force. Sherman quickly put his men to work destroying Confederate military supplies. They also burned dozens of houses, leaving only the brick chimneys standing. Satisfied with the result, the troops laughingly renamed Jackson "Chimneyville."[10]

While Sherman was occupied at Jackson, Grant successfully fought the Battle of Champion's Hill. General Pemberton's shaken Confederates fell back to a new defensive line on the Big Black River.

*Sherman's troops first fought those of Confederate General Joseph Johnston in Mississippi in 1863. The two generals would battle many times during the next two years.*

Sherman's XV Corps reached the Big Black River in time to help Grant defeat the Confederates again in another clash on May 17. Pemberton finally retreated to his defenses inside Vicksburg.

## The Siege of Vicksburg

On May 19, 1863, General Grant's entire army charged the Vicksburg defenses. The Union attack was driven back with heavy losses. Grimly Grant ordered a second attack on May 22. "The enemy rose behind their [defenses] and poured a furious fire upon our lines," Sherman remembered, "and, for about two hours, we had a severe and bloody battle."[11] Having failed twice to capture the town by assault, Grant decided to starve the enemy into surrender. While the rest of the army surrounded Vicksburg, Sherman marched 20 miles east with seven divisions back to the Big Black River. It was his task to prevent

General Johnston's twenty thousand Confederates from coming to the aid of Vicksburg.

For an entire month, Grant's artillery bombarded Vicksburg. Inside the town, Southern soldiers and citizens burrowed underground to escape the exploding shells. At last, when food ran out, General Pemberton admitted defeat. On July 4, 1863, he surrendered his entire army of thirty thousand men. Four days later, Union Major General Nathaniel Banks captured Port Hudson, Louisiana, about 150 miles farther down the river. The Mississippi River had been won. Northerners cheered, and Lincoln gladly announced to the nation, "The Father of Waters again goes unvexed to the sea."[12]

## A Second March to Jackson

Grant gave Sherman little time to enjoy the thrilling Vicksburg victory. He ordered him at once to attack Johnston's army. On July 6, Sherman began his march. Through heat and dust, his troops pursued Johnston all the way to Jackson and forced him to abandon the city on July 16. Union soldiers again set to work destroying everything of military value in the Mississippi capital. Factories, railroad shops, and warehouses crashed in burning ashes. "Jackson, once the pride and boast of Mississippi," Sherman declared, "is a ruined town."[13]

The tired XV Corps was finally rewarded with several weeks' rest in camps on the Big Black River. In August 1863, Ellen Sherman arrived with four of the Sherman children, Minnie, Lizzie, Willie, and Tom. "Willie was then nine years old . . .," Sherman proudly recalled. "He was a great favorite with the soldiers, and used to ride with me on horseback in the numerous drills and reviews of the time."[14] It was a brief period of relaxation for Sherman in the midst of bloody war.

# 6

# COMMANDER OF THE ARMY OF THE TENNESSEE

The North named its armies after important rivers. The Union Army of the Cumberland suffered a major defeat at the Battle of Chickamauga in Georgia in September 1863. Confederate General Braxton Bragg pursued the beaten army to Chattanooga, Tennessee. The Confederates camped on the heights of Missionary Ridge overlooking the city. General Bragg believed it was only a matter of time before the Union Army of the Cumberland must surrender.

In October, President Lincoln appointed Ulysses S. Grant overall general in the West, commanding the Union armies of the Cumberland, the Ohio, and the Tennessee. Grant selected Sherman to take his place in command of the Army of the Tennessee.

## A Family Tragedy

Grant instructed Sherman to bring the Army of the Tennessee to Chattanooga as quickly as possible to aid in the defense of that city. Beside the Big Black River, twenty thousand soldiers hurriedly loaded wagons. The roads north were soon thick with marching men. In Vicksburg, Sherman and his family boarded the steamboat *Atlantic* and started upriver for Memphis.

As the steamboat passed Young's Point, Sherman noticed how pale his son Willie had become. Army doctors aboard the boat recognized the boy's illness as typhoid fever. The family landed at Memphis on October 2, but sadly Willie died the next day. For days, Sherman was tortured by the thought that he might have taken better care of his dear son. "Sleeping, waking, everywhere I see poor little [Willie]," he said, grieving.[1]

## The Attack at Colliersville

Sherman could not mourn his personal loss for long. On October 11, he started for Chattanooga on a special train loaded with his headquarters staff. At Colliersville, Tennessee, soldiers stopped the train with a warning. A large force of Confederate cavalry was approaching. Sherman and the soldiers on the train, as well as the local garrison, took cover. They crouched behind the trees and rocks on the hill overlooking the railroad station. For four hours, Sherman with only six hundred men fought off the attacks of eight thousand rebel horsemen.

At one point, the Confederates succeeded in boarding the train. They captured several of the headquarters' staff horses, including Sherman's favorite horse, Dolly. Sherman's men kept firing from the hill above the tracks. "I was somewhat frightened at first," declared the train conductor, "but when I saw [General Sherman] so unconcerned amid all the [bullets] flying around him, I did not think it worthwhile for me to be scared."[2] Late in the afternoon, a division of four thousand Union troops finally arrived and drove away the attackers.

## The Battle of Chattanooga

On November 14, 1863, Sherman reached Chattanooga. Bragg's Confederates still held the high ground of Missionary Ridge. Chattanooga, with the Tennessee River behind it and the enemy in front of it, was besieged. Grant instructed Sherman to get his troops across the Tennessee River and attack Bragg's right flank on the northern end of Missionary Ridge. On the night of November 23, Sherman's army

engineers built a pontoon bridge 1,350 feet long. In
the morning, three divisions crossed.

Sherman promptly attacked what he thought was
the north end of Missionary Ridge. His soldiers soon
discovered, however, the slope was only a separate
hill at the end of the ridge. With determination,
Sherman continued his attack on Missionary Ridge
on November 25. From the heights above,
Confederate riflemen and cannoneers poured down
a terrible rain of shot and shell.

Sherman's West Point classmate Major General
George H. Thomas commanded the Army of the
Cumberland at the center of the Union line. While
Sherman's Army of the Tennessee kept up the fight
on the enemy's right, the Cumberland troops
charged at the center.
They soon captured
the rifle pits at the
base of Missionary
Ridge. Without await-
ing further orders,

*Union General Ulysses S. Grant
(1822–1885) often relied on Sherman
to perform difficult tasks. At
Chattanooga, he ordered Sherman's
Army of the Tennessee to attack the
strong Confederate position on
Missionary Ridge.*

thousands of excited Cumberland men rose from the rifle pits and scrambled up the ridge. Sudden panic gripped the Confederates. "The Yankees were cutting and slashing," exclaimed Southern Private Sam Watkins, "and the cannoneers were running in every direction. . . . The whole army was routed."[3] At daylight on November 26, Sherman hurried his men in pursuit, sending back captured cannons and hundreds of stunned Confederate prisoners. The Battle of Chattanooga was a surprising Union victory.

## A Rescue and a Raid

Sherman read his new orders just four days later on November 30. He was directed to rush to Knoxville, Tennessee, and save the garrison there. "We learned that twelve thousand of our fellow-soldiers were [surrounded] in the mountain town," Sherman explained, ". . . that they needed relief. . . . This was enough—and it had to be done."[4] On December 6, after seven days of hard marching over icy winter roads, Sherman's troops reached Knoxville. He discovered the Confederates had retreated to Virginia the night before.

The exhausted Army of the Tennessee went into winter camps along the Tennessee River during the next few weeks. On February 1, 1864, Grant requested that Sherman return to Mississippi. He was to lead twenty thousand men from Vicksburg

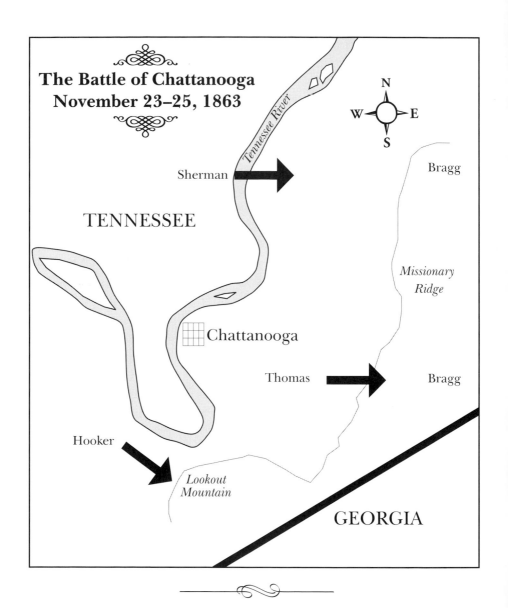

# The Battle of Chattanooga
## November 23–25, 1863

Tennessee River

N
W—E
S

Sherman

Bragg

TENNESSEE

Missionary
Ridge

Chattanooga

Thomas

Bragg

Hooker

Lookout
Mountain

GEORGIA

*While Sherman's troops engaged Bragg's Confederates' right flank, General George H. Thomas's Army of the Cumberland barreled through the center of the enemy line. The result was a surprising victory for the Union at the Battle of Chattanooga.*

through Jackson on a raid 130 miles east to the town of Meridian.

Sherman's infantry entered Meridian on February 14 without difficulty. The retreating Confederates had abandoned huge quantities of food, arms, clothing, and other supplies. Sherman's men promptly burned ten thousand bales of cotton and 2 million bushels of corn. During the next few days, they torched many city buildings and tore up over one hundred miles of railroad tracks. "Meridian, with its depots, store-houses, arsenals, hospitals, offices, [and] hotels . . . no longer exists," Sherman reported. "I have no hesitation in pronouncing the work as well done."[5]

# 7

# THE FIGHT FOR ATLANTA

Abraham Lincoln named Ulysses S. Grant general of all the armies of the United States in March 1864. As Grant rose in command, so did his trusted friend William Tecumseh Sherman. Grant placed Sherman in charge of all the Union armies in the West.

The Confederacy still had two powerful armies to be defeated. General Robert E. Lee commanded the Confederate army in Virginia, and General Joseph Johnston commanded the Southern troops in Georgia. Together Grant and Sherman settled on a simple plan. Sherman explained, "He was to go for Lee and I was to go for Joe Johnston."[1]

## From Dalton to Resaca

At his headquarters in Nashville, Tennessee, Sherman organized his grand army of nearly a hundred thousand men for his invasion of Georgia. Carefully he studied the 1860 census tables and tax reports of every county in the state. Sherman expected to live off the land. "Georgia has a million of inhabitants," he informed Grant. "If they can live, we should not starve."[2]

On May 6, 1864, clouds of dust rose into the air from the roads leading south into Georgia. Sherman's huge Western army was on the march. Johnston, with sixty-two thousand Confederates, held a strong defensive position in the mountains north of Dalton, Georgia. Instead of a direct attack, Sherman wisely made other plans. He would flank Johnston's position, swinging around the mountain range to capture Resaca, eighteen miles south of Dalton. Major General James B. McPherson, who now commanded the Army of the Tennessee, was ordered to seize the Atlantic and Western Railroad, Johnston's vital supply line.

By May 9, McPherson was just five miles from Resaca. "I've got Joe Johnston dead!" crowed Sherman.[3] But McPherson believed Resaca was too strongly defended. He failed to attack but fell back three miles to Snake Creek Gap instead. When next they met, Sherman said, "Well, Mac, you missed the opportunity of your life."[4]

## The Deadly Game of War

Sherman shifted more of his army and joined McPherson at Snake Creek Gap. Johnston realized he had to retreat from Dalton to meet the threat. Johnston hurried his army south, and on May 14, 1864, Sherman attacked the Confederates at Resaca. "Sherman's columns . . . moved in perfect step," exclaimed one Confederate officer, "with banners flying and bands playing, as though he expected to charm us."[5]

Johnston abandoned Resaca on the night of May 15. He crossed his troops to the south side of the Oostanaula River and then burned the bridges. That

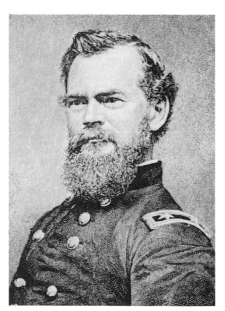

failed to stop Sherman's army engineers. They carried pontoon sections on their wagons. Transferred to the riverbank, tied side by side with ropes, and covered with

*As Sherman's trusted commander of the Army of the Tennessee, Union Major General James B. McPherson fought at Resaca, Georgia, in May 1864.*

planks, the pontoons soon became a useful bridge. Confederate soldier J. P. Austin declared, "Sherman [was] regarded by our boys as the champion bridge builder of the world."[6]

This was the Georgia region Sherman remembered so well from his visit in 1844 as a young lieutenant. "The thing that helped me to win battles in Georgia," he later remarked, "was my perfect knowledge of the country. I knew more of Georgia than the rebels did."[7] In their deadly game of cat and mouse, Johnston made a stand in the mountains at Allatoona Pass, fourteen miles below Resaca. Sherman skillfully sidestepped that easily defended position and marched southwest to New Hope Church near Dallas. He found the Confederates dug in behind breastworks of logs. On May 25, the two armies sharply clashed. "It was simply slaughter," one Union soldier recalled, ". . . hundreds of men surged right up to the breastworks and died there."[8] Within minutes, Sherman's army suffered nearly sixteen hundred dead and wounded. Still, Sherman forced Johnston's army back, nearer and nearer to Atlanta.

## Kennesaw Mountain

Johnston fell back on another strong defensive position. It was a chain of hills less than 30 miles north of Atlanta: Pine Mountain, Lost Mountain,

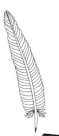

**Mother Bickerdyke**
Volunteer army nurse Mary Ann Bickerdyke was a middle-aged widow from Illinois. The troops fondly called her Mother Bickerdyke. She was the only woman Sherman allowed to travel with his army. Northern women sent her knitted socks, jars of fruit, and other welcome things, which she handed out to sick and wounded soldiers. One day in Georgia, army doctors complained to Sherman that Mother Bickerdyke was cluttering up their hospital with such items. Sherman only smiled and replied, "I can't do a thing in the world. She outranks me."[9]

and Kennesaw Mountain. This powerful position, as well as heavy rains, stopped Sherman for twenty-seven days.

On June 14, Sherman inspected his battle lines. On Pine Mountain half a mile away, he noticed a group of Confederate officers studying him through their binoculars. To General O. O. Howard, he commented, "How saucy they are. Howard, make 'em take cover. Have one of your batteries fire three volleys into 'em."[10] Howard ordered his cannons to fire, and the Confederate officers scattered. But Lieutenant General Leonidas Polk, one of

Johnston's corps commanders, moved too slowly. Polk was struck and instantly killed by a Union shell. During the next few days, Johnston gave up Pine Mountain and Lost Mountain. He concentrated his defenses on 700-foot-high Kennesaw.

On June 27, 1864, Sherman finally sent thirteen thousand men charging up Kennesaw Mountain. "The air seemed filled with bullets," one Union survivor recalled, "giving the sensation of moving swiftly against a heavy wind and sleet storm."[11] Cannonballs and musket bullets smashed into the blue lines. A Southerner remembered that Sherman's troops "seemed to walk up and take death as coolly as if they were automatic or wooden men."[12] In less than an hour, three thousand Union soldiers lay dead or wounded, while the Confederates lost fewer than a thousand men. The frontal assault at Kennesaw Mountain had been a failure.

## Within Sight of Atlanta

Sherman grimly ordered General McPherson to swing around Kennesaw Mountain and push southward. Johnston realized he was being outflanked again. He pulled off Kennesaw Mountain on July 2 and retreated to the southern bank of the Chattahoochee River. Sherman arrived at the

*In a drawing by Civil War artist Alfred Waud, Confederate Lieutenant General Leonidas Polk is struck by a Union cannon shell on Pine Mountain on June 14, 1864. In truth, the shell cut Polk's body into gory pieces.*

riverbank within days, eager to continue the attack. Union Major James A. Connolly remembered,

> I watched . . . Sherman stepping nervously about, his eyes sparkling and his face aglow—casting a single glance at Atlanta, another at the River, and a dozen at the surrounding valley to see where he could best cross the River, how he best could flank them.[13]

Sherman's expert army engineers swiftly constructed a 900-foot-long bridge. As Sherman's men crossed the river, Johnston retreated again, to within five miles of Atlanta.

## The Battle of Peachtree Creek

In Virginia, General Grant's brutal attacks on General Lee's Confederate defenses outside Richmond and Petersburg cost the lives of thousands of Union soldiers. Northerners grew depressed as the war dragged on. "Why don't Grant and Sherman do something?" wrote one weary New Yorker in his diary.[14] Confederate President Jefferson Davis felt General Johnston was not doing enough, either. On July 17, 1864, he replaced Johnston with Major General John Bell Hood. Union General John Schofield had been Hood's classmate at West Point. He remembered Hood as a headstrong, wild cadet. When Sherman asked what they could now expect, Schofield answered, "This means a fight. Hood will attack you within twenty-four hours."[15]

On the morning of July 20, the Confederates did indeed attack, pouring out of the forest at Peachtree Creek. Furiously they fell upon General George H. Thomas's Army of the Cumberland, beating it backward. Sergeant Rice C. Bull of the 123rd New York Regiment recalled,

> On the sound of the first shot every man jumped to his feet and into line. There was no waiting for orders, the men knew what was required. . . . Meanwhile the musketry firing was coming closer and closer, the yells of the enemy louder and louder, and the bullets began to sing and whistle around us and through the trees over our heads.[16]

Only after hours of desperate fighting did the Confederates withdraw.

## The Battle of Atlanta

Hood's defeat at Peachtree Creek forced the Confederate Army back to less than a mile and a half from Atlanta. On July 22, Hood stubbornly attacked again. This time he struck hard at General McPherson's Army of the Tennessee. Galloping through the woods toward the sound of battle, McPherson mistakenly rode in among some enemy troops. The Confederates shot him dead from his horse as he tried to escape.

Throughout the long, hot, summer day, the Army of the Tennessee bravely fought off the Confederate attack. General Howard remembered,

"I had never till then seen Sherman with such a look on his face. His eyes flashed. He did not speak. He only watched the front [with] a concentrated fierceness."[17] Unable to break the Union line, Hood at last fell back. Across the battlefield, some ten thousand Northern and Southern soldiers lay killed and wounded in what came to be called the Battle of Atlanta.

## Atlanta Under Siege

At the end of July, Sherman's artillerymen began firing their cannons into Atlanta. A Southern cavalryman witnessed one bombardment. "Citizens were running in every direction," he remembered. "Terror-stricken women and children went screaming about the streets seeking some avenue of escape from hissing, bursting shells."[18] In the days that followed, the Yankee cannons sent shells whistling into the city at the rate of one every five minutes. Sherman telegraphed to General Halleck: "One thing is certain, whether we get inside of Atlanta or not, it will be a used-up community when we are done with it."[19]

In time, Sherman realized he would be unable to capture the city until he cut the only remaining railroad line bringing supplies to the Confederate Army. Major General O. O. Howard had taken McPherson's place in command of the Army of the

*Confederate General John Bell Hood (1831–1879) was always a fighter. In 1863, Hood's left arm was mangled at the Battle of Gettysburg. Two months later, he lost his right leg after the Battle of Chickamauga. In 1864, while stubbornly defending Atlanta, Hood sent many of his soldiers to their deaths.*

Tennessee. Sherman ordered Howard to swing his troops southwest of Atlanta and seize the tracks of the vital Macon & Western Railroad. Hood lashed out at Howard's advancing army near Ezra Church on July 28. Again, the rebels suffered heavy losses. "We slaughter them by the thousands," declared one Union officer, "but Hood continues to hurl his broken, bleeding battalions against our . . . lines with all the fury of a maniac."[20] Since taking command just eleven days earlier, Hood had lost twenty thousand men, a full third of his entire army.

## "Atlanta Is Ours and Fairly Won"

On August 25, 1864, Sherman withdrew more troops from in front of Atlanta. Confederates in the city believed he was retreating north. Instead,

Sherman marched south and joined Howard. By August 30, he confidently announced, "I have Atlanta as certainly as if it were in my hand!"[21] Two days later, Sherman attacked at Jonesboro, 20 miles south of Atlanta. A Mississippi artilleryman remembered, "It was a grand and fearful sight to see that great army coming like a monster wave to engulf us."[22] The Union troops attacked the enemy line with such fury that Sherman exclaimed, "They're rolling 'em up like a sheet of paper!"[23]

The Union success at Jonesboro cut the railroad line into Atlanta. Now Hood had no choice but to retreat. On September 3, 1864, the Confederates exploded their ammunition supplies and abandoned the city. When he learned the news, Sherman excitedly telegraphed north: "Atlanta is ours, and fairly won."[24]

The victory at Atlanta was one of the most important of the war. It meant the capture of one of the South's major railroad junctions and manufacturing centers. President Lincoln called for a day of national thanksgiving in honor of the glorious event. Across the North, cannons boomed and church bells rang in celebration. General Grant gratefully told Sherman, "You have accomplished the most gigantic undertaking given to any general in this war."[25]

## 8

# THE MARCH
# TO THE SEA

"**G**eneral Sherman is the most American looking man I ever saw," described Union Major John Chipman Gray, "tall and lank . . . with hair like thatch, which he rubs up with his hands, a rusty beard trimmed close, a wrinkled face [and] small bright eyes. . . ."[1] Sherman dressed in a common soldier's uniform, without the fancy gold braid and red sash of a general. He wanted to be comfortable and was not concerned about looking important. Instead of riding boots, he wore low-cut shoes. Everything Sherman did he did with energy. He was in constant motion and always talking. "Nothing was more exciting than having Sherman enter a room," declared another officer, "and nothing was more relaxing than having him leave."[2]

## Total War

Sherman decided to make Atlanta a military fort. He instructed Mayor James M. Calhoun that Atlanta citizens must leave their homes. They could choose to travel either north or south. About half of the remaining three thousand people in Atlanta left the city. Wagons piled high with women and children, dogs, cats, and household furniture rolled away along the muddy streets. "If the people raise a howl against my . . . cruelty," Sherman plainly stated, "I will answer that war is war and not popularity-seeking. If they want peace, they and their relatives must stop the war."[3]

During the month of October 1864, Sherman chased Hood's forty-thousand-man Confederate army across northern Georgia. "To pursue Hood is folly," he finally declared, "for he can twist and turn like a fox and wear out any army in pursuit."[4] Sherman sent Generals George H. Thomas and John Schofield north with enough troops to defend Tennessee. For the rest of his soldiers, he had other plans. Sherman telegraphed Grant that he wanted to destroy Atlanta and then march southeast across Georgia all the way to Savannah. "I could cut . . . the

*A Union soldier is seen here resting on sandbags that were part of the Atlanta defenses. In September 1864, Sherman decided to make the entire city a military fort.*

Confederacy in two," he declared.[5] Within days, Grant gave his approval.

Sherman divided his sixty-two thousand soldiers into two wings. Major General O. O. Howard would command the right wing, containing the XV and the XVII corps. Major General Henry Slocum would lead the left wing with the XIV and the XX corps. Sherman ordered his soldiers to travel lightly. He expected them to live off the land. "There are rumors that we are to cut loose and march south to the ocean," commented Private Theodore Upson.

"We are in fine shape and I think could go anywhere Uncle Billy would lead."[6]

Sherman's troops set fire to Atlanta on the night of November 15. They would leave nothing behind of value to the enemy. By dawn of November 16, much of the city lay in ashes as the army started south. Sherman and his staff rode beside Howard's long marching column. "Atlanta was soon lost behind the screen of trees," Sherman described, "and became a thing of the past."[7] The troops strode along in a happy mood. These hardy veterans were eager for adventure. Private Upson proudly noted, "I doubt if such an army as we have ever was got together before . . . all the boys are ready for a meal or a fight and don't seem to care which it is."[8]

## The March Through Covington

On the second day of the march, Sherman's troops reached the town of Covington. "The street in front of our house was a moving mass of bluecoats," a young Covington woman named Allie Travis recalled, "—infantry, artillery, and cavalry—from 9 o'clock in the morning to a late hour at night."[9]

That evening, Sherman camped at a plantation outside of town. In the yard of the house, he chatted with an old, gray-haired slave. "I asked him if he understood about the war and its progress," Sherman recalled, and the old man said he did.

"Though [the North claimed] to be fighting for the Union, he supposed that slavery was the cause, and that our success was to be his freedom."[10]

Although Sherman tried to discourage them, in the days that followed, thousands of excited slaves, freed by the advancing army, joined Sherman's marching blue columns. "Wherever Sherman rode," wrote Massachusetts colonel Adin B. Underwood, "they crowded about him shouting and praying."[11] Although he was against slavery, Sherman sometimes grew upset when these people slowed down his march.

## Sherman's Bummers

Rich farmland covered the central Georgia landscape, and Sherman's army took advantage of the bountiful autumn harvest. Each morning, squads of soldiers scurried away from their brigades and searched for food. As they plundered the Georgia countryside, these soldiers were given the nickname "bummers."

Dolly Hunt Burge never forgot the bummers who swept onto her farm. "Like demons they rush in!" she said. "To my smoke-house, my dairy, pantry, kitchen, and cellar, like . . . wolves they come, breaking locks and whatever is in their way. The thousand pounds of meat in my smoke-house is gone in a twinkling, my flour, my meat, my lard, butter, eggs, pickles, wine are all gone. My . . . hens,

*One of Sherman's bummers is pictured carrying off food he has looted from a Georgia farm. Sherman's troops ate better on his march through Georgia than at any other time during the war.*

chickens, and fowls, my young pigs are shot down in my yard."[12] Each evening, the bummers returned to their brigade camps carrying plenty of supplies.

The army marched at the relaxed pace of about ten miles a day. This gave the soldiers time to tear up the Georgia railroads. "The track was heaved up in sections . . .," Sherman explained, "then . . . bonfires were made of the ties and of fence-rails on which the rails were heated, carried to trees or telegraph-poles, wrapped around and left to cool. Such rails could not be used again."[13] The soldiers laughingly referred to the twisted iron rails as Sherman's Bowties, Sherman's Corkscrews, and Sherman's Hairpins.[14]

## The Capture of Milledgeville

From Mississippi, Confederate General P.G.T. Beauregard sent an urgent appeal to Georgians: "Arise for the defense of your native soil! . . . Rally around your patriotic Governor and gallant soldiers. Obstruct and destroy all the roads in Sherman's front, flank, and rear, and his army will soon starve in your midst."[15] In fact, fewer than ten thousand Southern troops stood between Sherman's army and Savannah. Union soldiers easily defeated an attack by Georgia militiamen at Griswoldville on November 22.

On the rainy day of November 23, the left wing of Sherman's army entered Milledgeville, the capital of Georgia in 1864. In the abandoned state capital building, drunken Union soldiers held a mock legislative session. With comic speeches, they pretended to vote the state back into the Union. Growing more wild, they flung hundreds of books belonging to the state library out of the windows. In the yard below, soldiers snatched up volumes as souvenirs and trampled the rest into the mud.

**The World Awaits**

After leaving Atlanta, no news of Sherman reached the North. During a visit to the White House, John Sherman asked President Lincoln if he knew where his brother was heading. Lincoln answered, "I know the hole he went in at, but I can't tell you what hole he will come out of."[16] Another politician, A. K. McClure of Pennsylvania, visited Lincoln another day. "McClure," asked Lincoln, "wouldn't you like to hear something from Sherman?" McClure replied that he certainly would. "Well, I'll be hanged if I wouldn't myself," Lincoln replied.[17]

## The Attack on Fort McAllister

"The weather was fine, the roads good, and every thing seemed to favor us," Sherman later remembered.[18] During the first days of December 1864, his army entered the sandy, swampy region of southern Georgia. Soldiers began to sniff the salty air of the sea. Soon Fort McAllister on the Ogeechee River south of Savannah was all that kept the army from reaching Union supply ships waiting on the Georgia coast. On December 13, Sherman ordered Brigadier General William Hazen's 2nd Division of the XV Corps to capture the fort. They were the same troops Sherman had commanded at Shiloh and Vicksburg.

Sherman and several officers climbed to the roof of a rice mill to witness the attack. Hazen's men advanced out of the woods and moved steadily forward. Cannons in the fort belched fire, and the men suddenly charged. When the smoke cleared away, cheering blue-clad soldiers stood on the battlements waving a U.S. flag. "It's my old division," shouted Sherman. "I knew they'd do it!"[19] The next day the Union supply boats began bringing ashore food, clothing, and even sacks of mail.

*A view of the Savannah, Georgia, riverfront. Sherman presented the captured city to President Abraham Lincoln as an 1864 Christmas gift.*

## A Christmas Gift

Confederate General William Hardee abandoned Savannah in the early morning of December 21. With ten thousand troops, he escaped across the Savannah River into South Carolina. The next day Sherman triumphantly entered the captured city. He soon sent a glad message north to President Lincoln: "I beg to present you as a Christmas gift, the city of Savannah, with one hundred and fifty heavy guns and plenty of ammunition, also about twenty-five thousand bales of cotton."[20]

Altogether, Sherman's march through Georgia had left a path of ruin 60 miles wide and 300 miles long. In less than a month, he had kept his promise to slice the Confederacy in two. Burned mills, factories, and farms lay behind, an awful reminder of Sherman's tough new style of warfare. He made no apologies for his strategy. "We are not only fighting armies," he insisted, "but a hostile people, and must make old and young, rich and poor, feel the hard hand of war."[21]

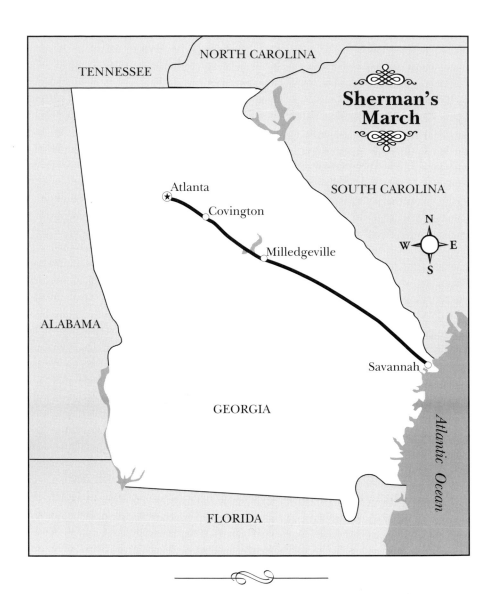

*With his three-hundred-mile march to Savannah, Georgia, Sherman and his bummers succeeded in cutting the Confederacy in two by tearing up train tracks and capturing or burning Confederate supplies. He then turned his sights on the Carolinas.*

# INTO THE CAROLINAS

Through the winter of 1864–1865, General Grant kept a close grip on Lee's defensive lines at Richmond and Petersburg, Virginia. In Savannah, Sherman busily prepared for his next campaign. He planned to march north through the Carolinas and continue to tear up the Confederate countryside. President Lincoln observed, "Grant has the bear by the hind leg while Sherman takes off its hide."[1]

## The South Carolina Swamps

On January 10, 1865, Sherman started soldiers marching inland from the South Carolina coast. To the Confederates, it looked as though he would attack Charleston. At the same time, Union troops crossed the Savannah River north of Savannah and seemed to threaten Augusta, Georgia. Sherman attacked neither place. Instead he directed most of his army northward into South Carolina's low-country swamps.

It was hard marching in wet weather. Rain fell almost constantly, and the troops regularly waded through knee-deep water. Some nights, guards patrolled their campsites by paddling canoes. One evening, a New York *Herald* reporter discovered a corps headquarters staff perched in the upper branches of a tree to escape the water. "Hello, old fellow," called Corps Commander Alpheus Williams. "You'd better come up and get yourself a roost."[2]

To build wagon roads through the swamps, Sherman relied on his pioneer corps. Four thousand soldiers and twenty-six hundred freed slaves swung shovels and axes. General Williams declared, "We became expert road-makers, first piling on all the fence rails and then cutting [down] young pines."[3] Wooden roads constructed in this fashion were called corduroy roads. Confederate General Johnston learned that Sherman's men were advancing through the swamps at the astonishing rate of ten miles a day. "I made up my mind," he later exclaimed, "that there had been no such army in existence since the days of [Roman general] Julius Caesar."[4] On February 9, 1865, the army reached

Union soldiers wade through the South Carolina swamps. This drawing appeared in Harper's Weekly, a popular magazine read by many Northerners during the Civil War.

dry land at last. Leaving the swamps behind, it headed toward the state capital of Columbia.

## "The Smokey March"

"When I go through South Carolina," Sherman had predicted, "it will be one of the most horrible things in the history of the world. The devil himself couldn't restrain my men in that state."[5] Many Union soldiers blamed South Carolina, the first state to secede, for starting the war.

Once, Sherman's cavalry general Judson Kilpatrick asked how he should let Sherman know where he was. Sherman answered, "Oh, just burn a bridge or something and make a smoke, as the Indians do on the plains."[6] Cavalry raiders set fires wherever they went. Kilpatrick later joked that he had changed the name of one South Carolina town from Barnwell to Burnwell.

Sherman's bummers kept busy, too. They torched farmhouses, barns, and piles of railroad ties. Bales of cotton and acres of pine trees all went up in flames. The soldiers called it "The Smokey March." "I think I shall never see a distant column of smoke rising hereafter, but it will remind me of Sherman," one Union officer said.[7]

## The Burning of Columbia

On February 17, Colonel George A. Stone's brigade of Iowa troops entered Columbia and received the mayor's surrender. By the time Sherman rode into the city later that day, it was already on fire. "Near the market-square we found Stone's brigade halted," Sherman recalled, "with arms stacked, and a large detail of his men, along with some citizens, engaged with an old fire-engine, trying to put out the fire in a long pile of burning cotton-bales."[8]

Perhaps retreating Confederates had started the blaze. Perhaps drunken Union soldiers were responsible. But Sherman went to bed believing the fire was under control. By eleven o'clock, however, the brightness of the flames outside awakened him. High winds had carried burning cinders onto dozens of houses. Sherman hurried outside and began shouting orders. Soldiers climbed onto rooftops with buckets of water to douse the spreading fire.

In the streets, men cursed and women and children wailed with terror. Soldiers and citizens worked feverishly side by side. "The whole air was full of sparks and of flying masses of cotton, shingles, etc.," Sherman described.[9] It was nearly dawn before the fire was brought under control. By then, about half of Columbia lay in smoldering ruins. Sherman offered no regrets for the destruction. "Though I never ordered it and never wished it," he said, "I have never shed many tears over the event, because I believe that it hastened what we all fought for, the end of the war."[10]

## On to North Carolina

The advancing army reached Cheraw, South Carolina, on February 19. There Sherman learned that his old enemy Joseph Johnston had taken command of the Confederate troops in North Carolina. After resting his army for three weeks, Sherman crossed the border into the state. "South Carolina has had a visit from the West that will cure her of her pride and boasting," he wrote to his wife.[11] Now it was North Carolina's turn to suffer the hard reality of war.

The constant terror of Sherman's marching army was felt throughout the Confederacy. Disheartened Southern soldiers deserted in growing numbers. "The simple fact that a man's home has been visited by an enemy," Sherman remarked with satisfaction, "makes a soldier in Lee's or Johnston's army very, very anxious to get home to look after his family and property."[12] In lovely spring weather, Sherman's troops crossed the Cape Fear River and entered Fayetteville, North Carolina, on March 11. They tramped ahead toward Goldsboro where Sherman expected to link up with General Schofield's corps, which was marching inland from the coast.

## Johnston Puts Up a Fight

On March 16, 1865, Johnston's Confederates clashed with the bluecoats at Averasboro. The brief fight hardly slowed the Union advance. By March 18, Sherman was within 25 miles of Goldsboro. He hoped that Johnston would retreat without another fight. On the night of March 19, however, General Slocum reported his left wing troops were under heavy attack at Bentonville. Through the next day, Slocum's half of the army fiercely defended itself, until Sherman arrived with reinforcements from Howard's right wing.

On March 21, Major General Joseph Mower sent his Union division charging into the rebels. They punched a hole in the Confederate battle line and nearly reached a bridge that would have prevented Johnston's retreat. Sherman, however, ordered them to halt before they reached their goal. "I think I made a mistake there," he admitted years later, "and should rapidly have followed Mower's lead with the whole of the right wing."[13]

Johnston's beaten army retreated again, unable to stop Sherman's northward march. The Union Army successfully entered Goldsboro on March 23. They were greeted by Schofield's XXIII Corps and tons of fresh supplies. The campaign was over. Sherman's remarkable winter march through the Carolinas had covered 425 miles in fifty days.

## Meetings Aboard the River Queen

A steamboat docked on the James River on the afternoon of March 27, 1865. Sherman had traveled up from North Carolina to discuss military plans with General Grant at his City Point, Virginia, headquarters.

"How d'you do, Sherman!" Grant called out.

"How are you, Grant!" shouted Sherman.

With glad smiles, the two men shook hands. "Their encounter," a witness observed, "was . . . like that of two schoolboys coming together after a vacation."[14]

President Lincoln was just then visiting Grant's army at City Point. Together, Grant and Sherman called on Lincoln aboard the steamboat *River Queen*. Four years of war had aged Lincoln. "When at rest or listening," Sherman noticed, "his legs and arms seemed to hang almost lifeless, and his face was care-worn and haggard."[15] Lincoln, however, eagerly listened to Sherman's description of the great marches. He laughed at Sherman's tales of the bummers and their methods of getting food.

Grant and Sherman visited a second time the following day. The president and his two valued generals decided that Grant should attack Lee at Richmond and Petersburg and that Sherman should continue his march north against Johnston. The end of the war, they all agreed, was certainly near. It was clear to Sherman during their talks that Lincoln wished to show the Southerners kindness once they had surrendered.

## A Tragic Telegram

Sherman returned by steamboat down the Atlantic Coast. He arrived at his Goldsboro, North Carolina, headquarters on March 31. With the addition of Schofield's corps, Sherman now had a force of eighty-nine thousand men. On April 10, the army started north, "straight against Joe Johnston wherever he may be," as Sherman said. "Poor North

Carolina will have a hard time, for we sweep the country like a swarm of locusts."[16]

The army's advance had barely begun when on April 12 Sherman received exciting news. General Robert E. Lee had surrendered his Confederate army to General Grant at Appomattox Courthouse, Virginia, on April 9. Sherman's soldiers threw their hats in the air and shouted for joy. Two days later, Johnston sent a message asking for a truce and a meeting with Sherman. The two generals arranged to meet midway between their armies.

On April 17, as Sherman was about to leave for this meeting, a telegrapher brought him an urgent message. It was from Secretary of War Edwin Stanton in Washington and was dated April 15. Sherman read the telegram with a sense of shock: "President Lincoln was murdered about 10 o'clock last night in his private box at Ford's Theatre in this city, by an assassin who shot him through the head with a pistol ball."[17]

Sherman quickly turned to the telegrapher.

"Has anybody else seen this?" he demanded.

"No."

"Then don't tell anyone—by word or look—until I return."[18] He feared his enraged soldiers might burn all of North Carolina to the ground if they found out the president had been killed.

A train carried Sherman to within five miles of the meeting place with Johnston. At Durham's Station, he left the train and rode forward with a cavalry escort toward the town of Hillsboro. On the road, he met Johnston riding with several Confederate officers.

## Surrender at Bennett's Farm

Rather than talk in the road, the two generals went to a small farmhouse nearby. James Bennett, the owner, gave them permission to use the house. As soon as they were alone, Sherman showed Johnston the telegram describing Lincoln's assassination. "The perspiration came out in large drops on his forehead," Sherman remembered, "and he did not attempt to conceal his distress."[19] Johnston admitted Lincoln's death was terrible news for all Americans.

Johnston realized his ragged army of twenty thousand men was no match for Sherman's huge, well-equipped army. He wished to surrender now with honor. He suggested, however, that instead of surrendering only his own army, they arrange terms that would include all of the Confederate armies still fighting. Sherman explained that he would need approval from Washington for such a broad surrender. But he clearly liked the idea. Major General John C. Breckinridge, who was Confederate Secretary of

*A view of the Bennett farmhouse. General Sherman and General Johnston discussed surrender terms here in April 1865. While waiting for news outside, Union cavalrymen fed their horses.*

War, was with Johnston's army. Johnston said he would confer with Breckinridge.

On April 18, Sherman and Johnston met a second time at the Bennett farmhouse. This time, Johnston brought Breckinridge with him, giving him the power to surrender all remaining Confederate armies. "Recalling the conversation of Mr. Lincoln, at City Point," Sherman later described, "I sat down at the table, and wrote off [surrender] terms, which I thought . . . expressed his views and wishes."[20] He handed the finished pages to Johnston, saying, "That's the best I can do."[21]

According to Sherman's terms, all Confederate soldiers were to give up their weapons at Southern arsenals and promise to obey federal authority again. No Confederate leaders would be punished as long as they obeyed federal laws. "We desire that you shall regain your position as citizens of the United States," Sherman explained, "free and equal to us in all respects."[22] Both Johnston and Sherman signed the document.

## Northern Reaction

On April 21, 1865, General Grant read Sherman's terms aloud at the White House to the new president, Andrew Johnson, and his Cabinet. When Grant finished, Secretary of War Stanton jumped to his feet and sharply accused Sherman of being far too generous. The entire Cabinet agreed that President Johnson must not approve Sherman's action. Many Northerners insisted that the South should be punished severely for both the war and the murder of Abraham Lincoln.

News of Sherman's surrender terms angered many people. Senator William Sprague of Rhode Island declared, "Loyal men . . . are outraged by Sherman's agreement with Johnston. He should be promptly removed."[23] The New York *Herald* exclaimed, "Sherman has fatally blundered, for, with a few unlucky strokes of his pen, he has blurred all the triumphs of his sword."[24]

Stanton issued a public statement criticizing Sherman's surrender terms. He let it be known that General Halleck, the army chief of staff, mistrusted Sherman. Confederate President Jefferson Davis was fleeing southward from Richmond, and Stanton spread rumors Davis might bribe Sherman with gold to let him escape.

## A New Treaty

General Grant was ordered south to take charge of the surrender negotiations. He arrived at Raleigh, North Carolina, on April 24. Grant told Sherman that his surrender terms had been rejected. He kept silent about Stanton's personal attacks on him. Sherman dutifully met with Johnston again on April 26 at the Bennett house and signed a new set of surrender terms. This time, Sherman followed the simple terms Grant had given Lee. He supplied ten days' rations to each of Johnston's surrendered soldiers and enough horses and mules for them to plant their spring crops.

It was not until two days later that Sherman saw New York newspapers containing Stanton's suggestion that he might be a traitor. This was a charge much worse than the charge of insanity he had endured in 1861. Union General Carl Schurz saw

Sherman soon after he learned the news. "He paced up and down the room like a caged lion," Schurz remembered.[25] During May of 1865, Sherman's troops marched north across Virginia. By May 19, the army pitched camp near Alexandria, Virginia, just across the Potomac River from Washington, D.C. From his tent, Sherman angrily sent word that the newspapers should be given notice "that the vandal, Sherman, is encamped near the canal bridge . . . where his friends, if any, can find him. Though in disgrace, he is untamed and unconquered."[26]

## The Grand Review

To celebrate the end of the war, the government arranged a two-day parade of Union armies down Pennsylvania Avenue. The great Eastern Army of the Potomac marched on May 23, 1865. At nine o'clock

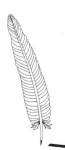

### Confederates on the Run

Confederate President Jefferson Davis escaped as far south as Irwinsville, Georgia. Union cavalrymen captured him there on May 10, 1865. Davis spent the next two years in a Northern prison. Lincoln's assassin, John Wilkes Booth, fled south, too. Cornered at last by Union cavalrymen near Bowling Green, Virginia, Booth was shot in the neck by Sergeant Boston Corbett and died on April 26.

*Sherman sat for this portrait with six of his most trusted generals in 1865. From left to right: O. O. Howard, John Logan, William Hazen, William T. Sherman, Jefferson C. Davis (no relation to Confederate President Jefferson Davis), Henry Slocum, and Joseph Mower.*

the next morning, it was the turn of Sherman's Western army to fall into marching formation. Sherman, with Major General O. O. Howard at his side, spurred his horse and headed the blue column down the broad avenue.

"Rap! rap! rap! down Pennsylvania Avenue," remembered Minnesota soldier Alonzo Brown. "The pavements are lined with spectators; boys as thick as locusts; windows crowded with ladies; roofs of the houses are jammed full of people."[27] People excitedly waved handkerchiefs and patriotic flags. They threw bouquets of flowers and cheered continuously.

"When I reached the Treasury-building and looked back," Sherman later recalled, "the sight was simply magnificent. The column was compact, and the glittering muskets looked like a solid mass of steel."[28]

Sherman rode past the reviewing stand in front of the White House and gave President Johnson a crisp salute. After passing, Sherman left the line of march. He dismounted his horse and entered the reviewing stand. He cheerfully shook hands with President Johnson and General Grant. Next in line, however, stood Edwin Stanton. When the Secretary of War held out his hand, Sherman coldly ignored it. Elbridge J. Copp, a war department telegrapher, saw the scene plainly: "Sherman's face was scarlet and his red hair seemed to stand on end."[29]

As a guest on the reviewing stand, for six and a half hours, Sherman proudly watched his army pass. "It was, in my judgment," he later declared, "the most magnificent army in existence—sixty-five thousand men. . . ."[30] These weathered Western soldiers had fought in six states. They had marched two thousand miles. "Many good people, up to that time," Sherman exclaimed, "had looked upon our Western army as a sort of mob; but the world then saw, and recognized the fact, that it was an army . . . well organized, well commanded and disciplined; and there was no wonder that it had swept through the South like a tornado."[31]

# 10

# FAITHFUL AND HONORABLE

"Let us all go to work and do what seems honest and just to restore our country," forty-five-year-old Sherman urged soon after the war ended.[1] Sherman chose to remain in the army. After the war, the U.S. government divided the South and the western territories into military districts, subject to army rule. In July 1865, Sherman was assigned command of the military district covering most of the American West from Ohio to the Rocky Mountains. He moved with his family to St. Louis, the district headquarters. A year later, he was promoted to the rank of lieutenant general.

## The Transcontinental Railroad

Sherman had long dreamed of seeing a railroad stretch from coast to coast. The Central Pacific Railroad began in 1865, building toward the East. At the same time, the Union Pacific Railroad began laying track from Omaha, Nebraska, westward. As work progressed on the Union Pacific, Sherman took monthly inspection tours. "Every time they build a section," he declared, "I'll be on hand to look at it and see that it is properly built."[2] During his trips, Sherman gave advice to General Grenville M. Dodge, chief builder of the railroad. He also assigned squads of soldiers to protect the work crews from American-Indian attacks.

Hundreds of army veterans worked on the Union Pacific. During Sherman's inspection rides, work crews waved their hats at his train. They shouted out the names of their old regiments and the battles where they had fought. They laughingly asked Sherman how he liked seeing them *build* a railroad.[3] In the summer and fall of 1866, Sherman toured as far west as Fort Laramie in the Wyoming Territory and Denver, Colorado. He loved to sit around the evening campfires. ". . . [H]e acted like a boy turned loose," remembered one companion, ". . . stretched in blankets before the fire in the shadow of mountains, he talked the night half away."[4]

Finally, on May 10, 1869, Sherman tore open a telegram from Promontory, Utah: "The tracks of the Union and Central Pacific Railroads were joined today," wrote General Dodge. "2,500 miles west of the Atlantic and 790 miles east of the Pacific Oceans."[5] The historic joining of these two railroads enabled rail travel across the entire nation for the first time. "The completion of the transcontinental railroad," Sherman exclaimed, "is as great a victory as any in the war."[6]

## Peace Commissioner

In August 1867, General Grant named Sherman a member of a commission established to try to bring

*Laborers build the Union Pacific Railroad in Nebraska in 1865. Many of these workers had been soldiers in Sherman's army.*

peace between settlers and American Indians in the West. The Peace Commission traveled to several places, including Fort Laramie in Wyoming. Sherman met there with leaders of the Cheyenne and Sioux tribes. Sherman held the view popular in the 1800s that American Indians were uncivilized and should be cleared off lands where white settlers could farm.

Sherman sat with the chiefs and gave them a stern warning. "We will build iron roads," he told them,

> and you cannot stop the locomotives any more than you can stop the sun or moon. . . . Our people . . . will come out as thick as the herd of buffaloes, and if you continue fighting you will all be killed. We now offer you this, choose your homes and live like white men and we will help you. . . . We will be kind to you if you keep the peace, but if you won't listen to reason we are ordered to make war upon you.[7]

In time, the commissioners signed a treaty with the Sioux, who agreed to live on lands set aside for them called reservations. By 1872, the Peace Commission also signed treaties with leaders of the Cheyenne, Navajo, Kiowa, Arapaho, and Comanche tribes. They all agreed to live peacefully on reservation lands.

## General of the Army

Americans elected General Grant the eighteenth president of the United States in 1868. When Grant took office, Sherman replaced him as head of the U. S. Army. The tall, lean, red-haired soldier proudly pinned on the four stars of a full general and moved to army headquarters in Washington, D.C.

As General of the Army, Sherman expected to have control of army organization. He was bitterly disappointed when President Grant permitted Secretary of War John Rawlins to deal directly with district commanders and other officers without consulting him. After Rawlins died in 1869, the new Secretary of War, W. W. Belknap, had the same power. Congress also interfered with the army. On July 7, 1870, it passed a law gradually shrinking the size of the army to just twenty-five thousand troops.

In early November 1871, Sherman took an opportunity to escape Washington politics. He boarded the USS *Wabash* and sailed for Europe. After landing in Spain, Sherman traveled to France, Italy, Turkey, Egypt, Russia, Germany, Austria, and Great Britain. Wherever he went, national leaders entertained the great American general at banquets and balls. In Turkey, Sherman witnessed a grand army review. The Turkish sultan then took him on a yacht trip into the Black Sea. In Switzerland, he visited Lake Zurich and the Alps. "I like American scenery better than any of it," Sherman honestly stated.[8] After a ten-month trip, he finally arrived back home in September 1872.

## St. Louis Headquarters

In 1874, Sherman moved army headquarters from Washington, D.C., to St. Louis, Missouri. He hated the political atmosphere of Washington. In St. Louis he could more closely guide army strategy and troop movements during the western American-Indian wars. He could also live more cheaply with his family there.

While living in St. Louis, Sherman completed writing his autobiography, which he had begun early in 1874. The book, *Memoirs of General William T. Sherman*, published by D. Appleton & Co. in March 1875, was a huge success. "If I had read my own books," remarked famed author Mark Twain, "half as many times as I have read those 'Memoirs,' I should be a wiser and better man than I am."[9] Mark Twain's publishing company, Charles L. Webster & Co., would publish a revised edition of Sherman's book in 1886.

In March 1876, Secretary of War Belknap resigned from office in disgrace for stealing army funds. As a result of the scandal, Sherman moved his headquarters back to Washington. President Grant named respected Judge Alphonso Taft the new secretary of war. Taft restored many of Sherman's powers as General of the Army.

## Sherman at Home

Sherman never forgot the men who had fought with him during the Civil War. He kindly responded to requests from needy veterans and their children. Almost daily, hungry old soldiers rang the Sherman doorbell. Out of his own pocket, he bought clothes and shoes for many penniless veterans, or railroad tickets so they could travel home.

In 1864, Ellen Sherman had given birth to a boy. Sadly, the infant Charles Sherman had died later that year. Philemon Tecumseh Sherman, the last of the eight Sherman children, was born in 1867. Two Sherman daughters, Minnie and Elly, married navy officers. Unmarried daughters, Lizzie and Rachel, remained at home.

Sherman's son Tom graduated from Yale University in 1876 and St. Louis Law School in 1878. Instead of becoming a lawyer, however, twenty-one-year-old Tom announced that he intended to study in England to become a Roman Catholic priest. Sherman was stunned by the news. He felt the Catholic Church had stolen his son from him. "My father, as you know," Tom told a relative, "is not a Catholic, and therefore the step I am taking seems . . . startling and . . . strange to him. . . . I go without his approval. . . . For he had formed other plans for me . . . and had other hopes and expectations in my regard."[10]

In August 1880, Father Tom Sherman returned home to the United States. Sherman greeted him with a loving hug. Tom happily reported, "Papa has let his grand heart get the best of past disappointment."[11]

## Sherman for President

On May 7, 1881, Sherman founded an advanced school of instruction at Fort Leavenworth, Kansas, for specially selected officers. It was called the School of Application for Infantry and Cavalry. He wanted future generations of army officers to have the best military knowledge possible. Two years later, on November 1, 1883, at the age of sixty-three, Sherman finally retired from the army. The Sherman family moved into a house at 912 Garrison Avenue in St. Louis.

Sherman, the heroic war general, was regarded as honest and trustworthy by most Americans, especially in the North. Sherman did not vote and never joined a political party. But every four years people suggested him as a Republican candidate for president. The hope of electing Sherman was greatest in 1884, the year after he retired. Just before the Republican convention that year, Maine congressman James G. Blaine wrote Sherman: ". . . it is more than possible . . . that you may be nominated. . . . [by] popular demand, and you can no more refuse than

*Sixty-four-year-old Sherman refused to run for president in 1884.*

you could have refused to obey an order when you were a lieutenant."[12]

In early June, Republican delegates assembled at Chicago. On June 5, delegate J. B. Henderson rushed to the telegraph office. Sherman's son Tom recalled, "I was at his side in his library on Garrison Avenue when he received the telegram. . . . 'Your name is the only one we can agree upon, you will have to . . . accept the Presidency.'"[13] Sherman had never liked politics and had vowed never to hold public office. Very calmly he wrote his definite answer to the important telegram: "I will not accept if nominated and will not serve if elected."[14] He gave the note to the messenger and thought nothing more about it. In Chicago, James G. Blaine finally won the nomination on the fourth ballot. Blaine lost the election to Democrat Grover Cleveland in November.

## The Old Army Veteran

The last years of Sherman's life were filled with banquets and public functions. Requests for speeches came from all over the country. To the secretary of a county fair at Rockford, Illinois, Sherman wrote on April 25, 1885: "Were you to see my mail for any three days . . . you would exclaim, 'For God's sake allow an old soldier some little rest.'"[15]

Each summer, Sherman attended veterans' reunions. With pride he held the office of president of the Society of the Army of the Tennessee from 1869 to 1891. He also returned often to West Point to take part in graduation ceremonies. Cadet Avery DeLano Andrews remembered, "His fine appearance in full dress uniform, his friendly advice and humorous [stories] of his own cadet days always made a deep impression. . . ."[16]

### "War Is Hell"

On August 11, 1880, at Columbus, Ohio, Sherman addressed a large crowd of veterans and civilians. "There is many a boy here today," he bluntly stated, "who looks on war as all glory, but, boys, war is all hell."[17] His words, shortened to "War is hell," in time became the most famous description of war ever uttered.

## "Wait for Me, Ellen."

The Sherman family moved to New York City in 1886. For the next two years they lived at the Fifth Avenue Hotel. Sherman often spent evenings at the Union League Club chatting with friends. He also enjoyed attending the opera, musical concerts, and plays.

In September 1888, the Shermans moved into a house at 75 West Seventy-first Street, close to Central Park. For years, Ellen Sherman's health had been failing. On November 28, 1888, Sherman sat reading in his basement office. Suddenly a hired nurse called down to him that his wife was dying. Stunned to hear this, Sherman ran up the stairs calling out, "Wait for me, Ellen, no one ever loved you as I love you."[18] He barely reached her bedside before she died. Ellen Sherman was buried in St. Louis beside her children Willy and Charles.

## Death of a Soldier

"With me the warfare is nearly ended," Sherman told friends in 1891, "and within a short time I shall join those who have gone before me."[19] On February 4, 1891, he caught a cold coming home from a theater party through a winter storm. During the next week, the cold developed into a serious fever. His brother John Sherman and his foster brother Tom Ewing hovered at his bedside. Repeatedly

Sherman asked that his gravestone read "Faithful and Honorable." Unable to breathe and overcome by fever, Sherman died on February 14, 1891, at the age of seventy-one.

In New York City, flags flew at half-mast. Thousands of mourners filed into the Seventy-first Street house to view the body. Crowds jammed the sidewalks outside when the coffin was finally brought out on February 19. Among the honorary pallbearers on that raw, icy day stood bareheaded eighty-two-year-old General Joseph Johnston. "General, please put on your hat," someone urged him, "you might get sick." Johnston refused. "If I were in his place," he simply replied, "and he were standing here in mine, he would not put on his hat."[20] This last show of respect would prove too much for the old Southern general. Ten days later, Johnston would die of pneumonia.

Sherman's coffin began a long journey west by railroad. Along the route, army veterans mournfully stood at attention as the train rolled past. At last the train reached St. Louis. Sherman was buried at Calvary Cemetery beside his wife and two children. Chiseled on his gravestone are the words "Faithful and Honorable."

At the time of Sherman's death, the *New York Herald* had declared, "He will live forever in the . . . hearts of a grateful people."[21] Even the Atlanta

*Constitution* stated, "When all is said that can be said, the fact looms up that this man was one of the greatest soldiers of the age."[22] During the Civil War, William Tecumseh Sherman taught the South the hard meaning of war. But his victories brought a swifter peace to a reunited and stronger nation.

# CHRONOLOGY

1820—Born in Lancaster, Ohio, on February 8, the son of Charles Sherman and Mary Hoyt Sherman.

1829—In June, his father dies; Tecumseh Sherman becomes the foster son of Thomas Ewing and Maria Ewing; Baptized as William Tecumseh Sherman.

1831—Foster father Thomas Ewing is elected to the U.S. Senate.

1832—Attends Lancaster Academy.

1834—Works as a surveyor in Ohio.
-1835

1836—Attends the United States Military Academy at
-1840  West Point, New York; Commissioned a second lieutenant in the U.S. Army on July 1, 1840.

1840—Serves at forts in Florida and Alabama;
-1842  Promoted to first lieutenant on November 30, 1841.

1842—Serves at Fort Moultrie in the harbor of
-1846  Charleston, South Carolina.

1846—War with Mexico declared in April; Serves as recruiting officer in Pittsburgh, Pennsylvania; In July, sails from New York City, New York, for duty in California.

1847—Arrives at Monterey, California, on January 26 and serves as quartermaster; Writes first official report on discovery of gold at Sutter's Mill.

1848—Mexican War ends with the signing of the Treaty of Guadalupe Hidalgo; Mexico gives up California and New Mexico territories.

1850—Returns East carrying military letters; Marries foster sister Ellen Ewing in Washington, D.C., on May 1; Promoted to the rank of captain in September and serves as commissary officer at Benton Barracks, Missouri, until 1853.

1853—Resigns from the army and manages Lucas &
–1857 Turner, a bank in San Francisco, California;
Briefly manages a bank in New York City in 1857.

1858—Works in Leavenworth, Kansas, as a real estate
agent.

1859—Serves as superintendent of the Louisiana
–1861 Military Seminary at Alexandria, Louisiana.

1861—Louisiana secedes from the United States on
January 26; Sherman returns North and becomes
president of the Fifth Street Railroad Company
in St. Louis, Missouri; Civil War begins after the
Confederate bombardment of Fort Sumter in
April; Sherman appointed colonel in the U.S.
Army in May; Fights at the Battle of Bull Run in
July; Promoted to brigadier general in August;
Becomes commander of the Kentucky military
department in October; Relieved of command
due to stress in November.

1862—Fights at Battle of Shiloh as a division commander
in April; Promoted to major general in May.

1863—Serves with General Ulysses S. Grant in the
fight to capture Vicksburg, Mississippi;
Confederate garrison at Vicksburg surrenders
on July 4; Son Willie dies of typhoid fever on
October 2; Becomes commander of the Army
of the Tennessee; Fights at the Battle of
Chattanooga in November.

1864—Leads raid on Meridian, Mississippi, in February;
Becomes commander of all U.S. armies in the
West in March; Fights to capture Atlanta,
Georgia, from May until September; Burns
Atlanta on November 15; Marches southeast
from Atlanta three hundred miles to Savannah,
Georgia; Captures Savannah on December 21.

1865—Marches north through the South Carolina
swamps, January–February; Occupies Columbia,
South Carolina, and continues north to North
Carolina, February–March; Fights Confederates

at Bentonville, North Carolina, on March 19–21; General Robert E. Lee surrenders his Confederate army to Ulysses S. Grant at Appomattox Courthouse, Virginia, on April 9; President Abraham Lincoln assassinated by John Wilkes Booth on April 14; General Joseph Johnston surrenders his Confederate army to Sherman at Bennett's farm near Durham, North Carolina, on April 26; Sherman's Western army marches in the Grand Review in Washington, D.C., on May 24; Named commander of the Western military district in July.

1866—Promoted to lieutenant general.

1867—Serves as peace commissioner and meets with American-Indian leaders.

1868—Becomes General of the Army.

1869—Transcontinental railroad completed on May 10.

1871—Travels in Europe for ten months.
–1872

1875—Publishes autobiography.

1881—Founds army school of instruction at Fort Leavenworth, Kansas.

1883—Retires from the army; Lives in St. Louis, Missouri.

1884—Refuses to run for president of the United States.

1886—Moves to New York City.

1888—Wife, Ellen, dies on November 28.

1891—Dies in New York City on February 4, 1891; Is buried at Calvary Cemetery in St. Louis, Missouri.

# CHAPTER NOTES

### Chapter 1. The Burning of Atlanta

1. Mills Lane, ed., *"War Is Hell!" William T. Sherman* (Savannah, Ga.: The Beehive Press, 1974), p. xix.

2. William T. Sherman, *Memoirs of General William T. Sherman* (Bloomington: Indiana University Press, 1957), vol. 2, p. 167.

3. Stanley P. Hirshon, *The White Tecumseh* (New York: John Wiley & Sons, Inc., 1997), p. 246.

### Chapter 2. The Foster Son

1. Lloyd Lewis, *Sherman: Fighting Prophet* (New York: Harcourt, Brace and Company, 1932), p. 32.

2. John F. Marszalek, *Sherman A Soldier's Passion for Order* (New York: The Free Press, 1993), p. 9.

3. Lewis, p. 34.

4. Ibid., p. 38.

5. Ibid., pp. 39–40.

6. Ibid., p. 33.

7. Marszalek, p. 12.

8. Lewis, p. 45.

9. Stanley P. Hirshon, *The White Tecumseh* (New York: John Wiley & Sons, Inc., 1997), p. 9.

10. Lewis, p. 48.

11. Ibid., p. 51.

12. Ibid., p. 56.

13. Hirshon, pp. 13–14.

### Chapter 3. Soldier and Civilian

1. Stanley P. Hirshon, *The White Tecumseh* (New York: John Wiley & Sons, Inc., 1997), p. 17.

2. John F. Marszalek, *Sherman A Soldier's Passion for Order* (New York: The Free Press, 1993), p. 50.

3. William T. Sherman, *Memoirs of General William T. Sherman* (Bloomington: Indiana University Press, 1957), vol. 1, p. 13.

4. Ibid., p. 18.

5. Marszalek, p. 67.

6. Sherman, p. 40.

7. Ibid., p. 78.

8. Lloyd Lewis, *Sherman: Fighting Prophet* (New York: Harcourt, Brace and Company, 1932), p. 87.

9. Marszalek, p. 94.

10. Sherman, pp. 113–114.

11. Hirshon, p. 51.

12. Marszalek, p. 114.

13. Lewis, p. 102.

14. Sherman, p. 140.

15. Mark Coburn, *Terrible Innocence* (New York: Hippocrene Books, 1993), p. 33.

16. Sherman, p. 143.

## Chapter 4. The Nation Torn in Two

1. Lloyd Lewis, *Sherman: Fighting Prophet* (New York: Harcourt, Brace and Company, 1932), pp. 126–127.

2. Ibid., p. 136.

3. William T. Sherman, *Memoirs of General William T. Sherman* (Bloomington: Indiana University Press, 1957), vol. 1, p. 168.

4. Richard Wheeler, *Voices of the Civil War* (New York: Penguin Books USA, Inc., 1976), p. 29.

5. Stanley P. Hirshon, *The White Tecumseh* (New York: John Wiley & Sons, Inc., 1997), p. 93.

6. Sherman, p. 187.

7. Ibid., p. 192.

8. Lewis, p. 192.

9. Sherman, p. 201.

10. Ibid., p. 203.

11. John F. Marszalek, *Sherman A Soldier's Passion for Order* (New York: The Free Press, 1993), p. 163.

12. Sherman, p. 214.

13. Hirshon, p. 103.

14. Mark Coburn, *Terrible Innocence* (New York: Hippocrene Books, 1993), pp. 40–41.

15. Lewis, p. 212.

16. James M. McPherson, *Battle Cry of Freedom* (New York: Oxford University Press, 1988), p. 409.

17. Lewis, p. 222.

18. Ulysses S. Grant, *Personal Memoirs of U. S. Grant* (New York: Charles L. Webster & Company, 1894), p. 203.

19. Marszalek, p. 180.

20. Ibid., p. 181.

21. Sherman, p. 215.

## Chapter 5. General of the XV Corps

1. Geoffrey C. Ward, *The Civil War* (New York: Alfred A. Knopf, Inc., 1990), p. 321.

2. John F. Marszalek, *Sherman A Soldier's Passion for Order* (New York: The Free Press, 1993), p. 183.

3. William T. Sherman, *Memoirs of General William T. Sherman* (Bloomington: Indiana University Press, 1957), vol. 1, p. 255.

4. Sherman, p. 282.

5. Marszalek, p. 207.

6. Sherman, p. 292.

7. Lloyd Lewis, *Sherman: Fighting Prophet* (New York: Harcourt, Brace and Company, 1932), pp. 270–271.

8. Stanley P. Hirshon, *The White Tecumseh* (New York: John Wiley & Sons, Inc., 1997), p. 152.

9. Lewis, p. 274.

10. James M. McPherson, *Battle Cry of Freedom* (New York: Oxford University Press, 1988), p. 630.

11. Sherman, p. 326.

12. Richard Wheeler, *Voices of the Civil War* (New York: Penguin Books USA Inc., 1976), p. 350.

13. Marszalek, p. 229.

14. Sherman, p. 345.

## Chapter 6. Commander of the Army of the Tennessee

1. Lloyd Lewis, *Sherman: Fighting Prophet* (New York: Harcourt, Brace and Company, 1932), p. 310.

2. John F. Marszalek, *Sherman A Soldier's Passion for Order* (New York: The Free Press, 1993), p. 239.

3. Sam Watkins, *Co. Aytch* (Wilmington, N.C.: Broadfoot Publishing Company, 1990), p. 125.

4. William T. Sherman, *Memoirs of General William T. Sherman* (Bloomington: Indiana University Press, 1957), vol. 1, p. 380.

5. Marszalek, p. 254.

## Chapter 7. The Fight for Atlanta

1. Lloyd Lewis, *Sherman: Fighting Prophet* (New York: Harcourt, Brace and Company, 1932), p. 345.

2. Mills Lane, ed., *"War Is Hell!" William T. Sherman* (Savannah, Ga.: The Beehive Press, 1974), p. 26.

3. Mark Coburn, *Terrible Innocence* (New York: Hippocrene Books, 1993), p. 82.

4. James M. McPherson, *Battle Cry of Freedom* (New York: Oxford University Press, 1988), p. 745.

5. The editors of Time-Life Books, *Voices of the Civil War— Atlanta* (Richmond, Va.: Time-Life Books, 1996), p. 44.

6. Lewis, p. 360.

7. Ibid., p. 368.

8. *Voices of the Civil War—Atlanta*, p. 54.

9. Coburn, p. 115.

10. Lewis, p. 373.

11. Jay Luvaas, "Kennesaw Mountain, Georgia, Cobb County, June 27, 1864," in Frances H. Kennedy, ed., *The Civil War Battlefield Guide* (Boston: Houghton Mifflin Company, 1998), p. 338.

12. Geoffrey C. Ward, *The Civil War* (New York: Alfred A. Knopf, Inc., 1990), p. 324.

13. *Voices of the Civil War— Atlanta*, p. 87.

14. McPherson, p. 750.

15. Stanley P. Hirshon, *The White Tecumseh* (New York: John Wiley & Sons, Inc., 1997), p. 228.

16. *Voices of the Civil War—Atlanta*, p. 98.

17. Hirshon, p. 232.

18. *Voices of the Civil War—Atlanta*, p. 90.

19. William T. Sherman, *Memoirs of General William T. Sherman* (Bloomington: Indiana University Press, 1957), vol. 2, p. 101.

20. Coburn, p. 105.

21. Ibid., p. 108.

22. *Voices of the Civil War—Atlanta*, p. 91.

23. Lewis, p. 406.

24. John F. Marszalek, *Sherman A Soldier's Passion for Order* (New York: The Free Press, 1993), p. 283.

25. Lewis, p. 410.

## Chapter 8. The March to the Sea

1. Mark Coburn, *Terrible Innocence* (New York: Hippocrene Books, 1993), pp. 113–114.

2. Ibid., p. 113.

3. Stanley P. Hirshon, *The White Tecumseh* (New York: John Wiley & Sons, Inc., 1997), p. 241.

4. Coburn, p. 155.

5. James M. McPherson, *Battle Cry of Freedom* (New York: Oxford University Press, 1988), p. 808.

6. Geoffrey C. Ward, *The Civil War* (New York: Alfred A. Knopf, Inc., 1990), p. 340.

7. William T. Sherman, *Memoirs of General William T. Sherman* (Bloomington: Indiana University Press, 1957), vol. 2, pp. 178–179.

8. Burke Davis, *Sherman's March* (New York: Random House, 1980), pp. 11–12.

9. Richard Wheeler, *Voices of the Civil War* (New York: Penguin Books USA, Inc., 1976), p. 427.

10. Sherman, pp. 180–181.

11. Hirshon, p. 256.

12. Mills Lane, ed., *"War Is Hell!" William T. Sherman* (Savannah, Ga.: The Beehive Press, 1974), p. xv.

13. Sherman, p. 105.

14. Hirshon, p. 256.

15. Davis, p. 50.

16. Lloyd Lewis, *Sherman: Fighting Prophet* (New York: Harcourt, Brace and Company, 1932), p. 458.

17. Ibid., p. 459.

18. Sherman, p. 193.

19. Lewis, p. 463.

20. Coburn, p. 185.

21. Lewis, p. 468.

## Chapter 9. Into the Carolinas

1. Lloyd Lewis, *Sherman: Fighting Prophet* (New York: Harcourt, Brace and Company, 1932), p. 485.

2. Burke Davis, *Sherman's March* (New York: Random House, 1980), p. 145.

3. Mark Coburn, *Terrible Innocence* (New York: Hippocrene Books, 1993), p. 198.

4. Frances H. Kennedy, ed., *The Civil War Battlefield Guide* (Boston: Houghton Mifflin Company, 1998), p. 411.

5. Geoffrey C. Ward, *The Civil War* (New York: Alfred A. Knopf, Inc., 1990), p. 356.

6. Stanley P. Hirshon, *The White Tecumseh* (New York: John Wiley & Sons, Inc., 1997), p. 279.

7. John F. Marszalek, *Sherman A Soldier's Passion for Order* (New York: The Free Press, 1993), p. 321.

8. William T. Sherman, *Memoirs of General William T. Sherman* (Bloomington: Indiana University Press, 1957), vol. 2, p. 280.

9. Ibid., p. 286.

10. Ward, p. 359.

11. Coburn, p. 208.

12. Davis, p. 210.

13. Coburn, p. 212.

14. Marszalek, p. 336.

15. Sherman, p. 328.

16. Davis, p. 247.

17. Ibid., p. 259.

18. Ibid.

19. Sherman, p. 349.

20. Ibid., p. 353.

21. Lewis, p. 540.

22. Ibid., p. 539.

23. Ibid., p. 552.

24. Ibid.

25. Hirshon, p. 310.

26. Lewis, p. 567.

27. Davis, p. 290.

28. Sherman, p. 377.

29. Lewis, p. 577.

30. Sherman, p. 377.

31. Ibid., p. 378.

## Chapter 10. Faithful and Honorable

1. Lloyd Lewis, *Sherman: Fighting Prophet* (New York: Harcourt, Brace and Company, 1932), p. 586.

2. Ibid., p. 595.

3. Mark Coburn, *Terrible Innocence* (New York: Hippocrene Books, 1993), p. 234.

4. Lewis, p. 596.

5. Ibid., p. 599.

6. John F. Marszalek, *Sherman A Soldier's Passion for Order* (New York: The Free Press, 1993), p. 393.

7. Lewis, p. 598.

8. Ibid., p. 612.

9. Coburn, p. 231.

10. Lewis, pp. 627–628.

11. Marszalek, p. 414.

12. Lewis, pp. 629–630.

13. Ibid., p. 631.

14. Ibid.

15. Ibid., p. 632.

16. Sidney Forman, *West Point* (New York: Columbia University Press, 1950), p. 146.

17. Stanley P. Hirshon, *The White Tecumseh* (New York: John Wiley & Sons, Inc., 1997), p. 372.

18. Lewis, p. 645.

19. Marszalek, p. 490.

20. Coburn, p. 241.

21. Marszalek, p. 494.

22. Ibid., p. 495.

# GLOSSARY

**artery**—A tube-shaped vessel that carries blood through the body.

**assault**—An attack.

**battalion**—A body of troops.

**batteries**—Groups of cannons.

**breastworks**—Temporary defenses.

**brigade**—A military unit consisting of two or more regiments.

**brigadier general**—An army rank above colonel but below major general.

**census**—A population count.

**cholera**—A deadly bacterial disease that affects the stomach and intestines.

**concentrate**—To bring together.

**corps**—A military unit consisting of two or more divisions.

**dispose**—To have a tendency.

**division**—A military unit consisting of two or more brigades.

**flank**—To approach from the side.

**foundry**—An establishment where metal is cast into useful shapes.

**junction**—A place where roads intersect.

**orderly**—A soldier assigned to serve as an assistant.

**pallbearer**—A person who helps carry a coffin at a funeral.

**plunder**—To take by force.

**quartermaster**—A military officer whose duty is to provide housing, clothing, and food for troops.

**regiment**—A military unit of one thousand troops or less.

**relentless**—Without giving up.

**saucy**—Bold.

**secede**—To withdraw from an organization.

**seminary**—An institution of learning.

**sultan**—The absolute ruler of an Islamic country.

**unvexed**—Unbothered; without hindrance.

**vital**—Of the greatest importance.

**wharf**—A waterside platform on which a ship's cargo may be loaded or unloaded.

# FURTHER READING

## Books

Arnold, James R. and Roberta Wiener. *Divided in Two.* Minneapolis: The Lerner Publishing Group, 2002.

Harmon, Dan. *Civil War Generals.* Broomhall, Pa.: Chelsea House Publishers, 1999.

Kennett, Lee B. *Marching Through Georgia.* New York: HarperTrade, 1995.

Remstein, Henna. *William Sherman: Union Military Leader.* Broomhall, Pa.: Chelsea House Publishers, 2000.

Whitelaw, Nancy. *William Tecumseh Sherman: Defender & Destroyer.* Greensboro, N.C.: Morgan Reynolds, Incorporated, 1996.

## Internet Addresses

Museum of the City of San Francisco. "Gen. William Tecumseh Sherman." © 1995–2001. <http://www.sfmuseum.org/bio/sherman.html>

The War Times Journal. "Memoirs: William T. Sherman." © 1997–1999. <http://www.wtj.com/archives/sherman/>.

The West Film Project and WETA. "William Tecumseh Sherman (1820–1891)." *New Perspectives on the West.* © 2001. <http://www.pbs.org/weta/thewest/people/s_z/sherman.htm>.

# INDEX